3124300 495 5679

Lake Forest Library
360 E. Deerpath
Lake Forest, IL 60045
847-234-0636
www.lakeforestlibrary.org

Think Complexity

Allen B. Downey

D1214138

O'REILLY®

Beijing · Cambridge · Farnham · Köln · Sebastopol · Tokyo

Think Complexity
by Allen B. Downey

Copyright © 2012 Allen Downey. All rights reserved.
Printed in the United States of America.

Published by O'Reilly Media, Inc., 1005 Gravenstein Highway North, Sebastopol, CA 95472.

O'Reilly books may be purchased for educational, business, or sales promotional use. Online editions are also available for most titles (*http://my.safaribooksonline.com*). For more information, contact our corporate/institutional sales department: (800) 998-9938 or *corporate@oreilly.com*.

Editors: Mike Loukides and Meghan Blanchette
Production Editor: Kristen Borg
Proofreader: Katie DePasquale

Indexer: Allen Downey
Cover Designer: Karen Montgomery
Interior Designer: David Futato
Illustrator: Robert Romano

March 2012:   First Edition.

Revision History for the First Edition:
    2012-02-21   First release
    2012-03-20   Second release
    2012-05-10   Third release
See *http://oreilly.com/catalog/errata.csp?isbn=9781449314637* for release details.

Think Complexity is available under the Creative Commons Attribution-NonCommercial-ShareAlike 3.0 Unported License (*http://creativecommons.org/licenses/by-nc-sa/3.0/legalcode*). The author maintains an online version at *http://thinkcomplex.com/thinkcomplexity.pdf*.

Nutshell Handbook, the Nutshell Handbook logo, and the O'Reilly logo are registered trademarks of O'Reilly Media, Inc. *Think Complexity*, the image of a black eagle, and related trade dress are trademarks of O'Reilly Media, Inc.

Many of the designations used by manufacturers and sellers to distinguish their products are claimed as trademarks. Where those designations appear in this book, and O'Reilly Media, Inc., was aware of a trademark claim, the designations have been printed in caps or initial caps.

While every precaution has been taken in the preparation of this book, the publisher and author assume no responsibility for errors or omissions, or for damages resulting from the use of the information contained herein.

ISBN: 978-1-449-31463-7

[LSI]

1336659947

Table of Contents

Preface

Why I Wrote This Book

This book is inspired by boredom and fascination: boredom with the usual presentation of data structures and algorithms, and fascination with complex systems. The problem with data structures is that they are often taught without a motivating context; the problem with complexity science is that it is usually not taught at all.

In 2005, I developed a new class at Olin College where students read about topics in complexity, implement experiments in Python, and learn about algorithms and data structures. I wrote the first draft of this book when I taught the class again in 2008.

For the third offering, in 2011, I prepared the book for publication and invited the students to submit their work in the form of case studies for inclusion in the book. I recruited nine professors at Olin to serve as a program committee and choose the reports that were ready for publication. The case studies that met the standard are included in this book. For the next edition, we invite additional submissions from readers (see Appendix A).

Suggestions for Teachers

This book is intended as a scaffold for an intermediate-level college class in Python programming and algorithms. My class uses the following structure:

Reading

    Complexity science is a collection of diverse topics. There are many interconnections, but it takes time to see them. To help students see the big picture, I give them readings from popular presentations of work in the field. My reading list and suggestions on how to use it are in Appendix B.

Exercises

    This book presents a series of exercises; many of them ask students to reimplement seminal experiments and extend them. One of the attractions of complexity is that the research frontier is accessible with moderate programming skills and undergraduate mathematics.

Discussion

The topics in this book raise questions in the philosophy of science, and lend themselves to further reading and classroom discussion.

Case studies

In my class, we spend almost half the semester on case studies. Students participate in an idea generation process, form teams, and work for 6–7 weeks on a series of experiments, which they then present in the form of a publishable 4–6 page report.

An outline of the course and my notes are available at *https://sites.google.com/site/comp modolin*.

Suggestions for Autodidacts

In 2009–10, I was a Visiting Scientist at Google, working in their Cambridge office. One of the things that impressed me about the software engineers I worked with was their broad intellectual curiosity and drive to expand their knowledge and skills.

I hope this book helps people like them explore a set of topics and ideas they might not encounter otherwise, practice programming skills in Python, and learn more about data structures and algorithms (or review material that might have been less engaging the first time around).

Some features of this book intended for autodidacts are:

Technical depth

There are many books about complex systems, but most are written for a popular audience. They usually skip the technical details, which is frustrating for people who can handle it. This book presents the mathematics and other technical content you need to really understand this work.

Further reading

Throughout the book, I include pointers to further reading, including original papers (most of which are available electronically), related articles from Wikipedia,[1] and other sources.

Exercises and (some) solutions

For many of the exercises, I provide code to get you started, and solutions if you get stuck or want to compare your code to mine.

---

1. Some professors have an allergic reaction to Wikipedia, on the grounds that students may depend too heavily on an unreliable source. Since many of my references are Wikipedia articles, I want to explain my thinking. First, the articles on complexity science and related topics tend to be very good; second, they are written at a level that is accessible after you have read this book (but sometimes not before); and finally, they are freely available to readers all over the world. If there is a danger in sending readers to these references, it is not that they are unreliable, but that the readers won't come back! (See *http://xkcd .com/903*.)

Opportunity to contribute

If you explore a topic not covered in this book, reimplement an interesting experiment, or perform one of your own, I invite you to submit a case study for possible inclusion in the next edition of the book. See Appendix A for details.

This book will continue to be a work in progress. You can read about ongoing developments at *http://www.facebook.com/thinkcomplexity*.

Allen B. Downey
Professor of Computer Science
Olin College of Engineering
Needham, MA

Contributor List

If you have a suggestion or correction, please send an email to downey@allendowney .com. If I make a change based on your feedback, I will add you to the contributor list (unless you ask to be omitted).

If you include at least part of the sentence the error appears in, that makes it easy for me to search. Page and section numbers are fine, too, but not quite as easy to work with. Thanks!

- Richard Hollands pointed out several typos.
- John Harley, Jeff Stanton, Colden Rouleau, and Keerthik Omanakuttan are computational modeling students who pointed out typos.
- Muhammad Najmi bin Ahmad Zabidi caught some typos.
- Phillip Loh, Corey Dolphin, Noam Rubin, and Julian Ceipek found typos and made helpful suggestions.
- José Oscar Mur-Miranda found several typos.
- I am grateful to the program committee that read and selected the case studies included in this book: Sarah Spence Adams, John Geddes, Stephen Holt, Vincent Manno, Robert Martello, Amon Millner, José Oscar Mur-Miranda, Mark Somerville, and Ursula Wolz.
- Sebastian Schöner sent two pages of typos!
- Jonathan Harford found a code error.
- Philipp Marek sent a number of corrections.

Conventions Used in This Book

The following typographical conventions are used in this book:

Italic

    Indicates URLs, email addresses, filenames, and file extensions.

Bold

    Indicates new terms.

`Constant width`

    Used for program listings, as well as within paragraphs to refer to program elements such as variable or function names, databases, data types, environment variables, statements, and keywords.

`Constant width bold`

    Shows commands or other text that should be typed literally by the user.

`Constant width italic`

    Shows text that should be replaced with user-supplied values or by values determined by context.

 This icon signifies a tip, suggestion, or general note.

 This icon indicates a warning or caution.

Using Code Examples

This book is here to help you get your job done. In general, you may use the code in this book in your programs and documentation. You do not need to contact us for permission unless you're reproducing a significant portion of the code. For example, writing a program that uses several chunks of code from this book does not require permission. Selling or distributing a CD-ROM of examples from O'Reilly books does require permission. Answering a question by citing this book and quoting example code does not require permission. Incorporating a significant amount of example code from this book into your product's documentation does require permission.

We appreciate, but do not require, attribution. An attribution usually includes the title, author, publisher, and ISBN. For example: "*Think Complexity* by Allen B. Downey (O'Reilly). Copyright 2012 Allen Downey, 978-1-449-31463-7."

If you feel your use of code examples falls outside fair use or the permission given above, feel free to contact us at *permissions@oreilly.com*.

Safari® Books Online

 Safari Books Online is an on-demand digital library that lets you easily search over 7,500 technology and creative reference books and videos to find the answers you need quickly.

With a subscription, you can read any page and watch any video from our library online. Read books on your cell phone and mobile devices. Access new titles before they are available for print, and get exclusive access to manuscripts in development and post feedback for the authors. Copy and paste code samples, organize your favorites, download chapters, bookmark key sections, create notes, print out pages, and benefit from tons of other time-saving features.

O'Reilly Media has uploaded this book to the Safari Books Online service. To have full digital access to this book and others on similar topics from O'Reilly and other publishers, sign up for free at *http://my.safaribooksonline.com*.

How to Contact Us

Please address comments and questions concerning this book to the publisher:

O'Reilly Media, Inc.
1005 Gravenstein Highway North
Sebastopol, CA 95472
800-998-9938 (in the United States or Canada)
707-829-0515 (international or local)
707-829-0104 (fax)

We have a web page for this book, where we list errata, examples, and any additional information. You can access this page at:

http://shop.oreilly.com/product/0636920022480.do

To comment or ask technical questions about this book, send email to:

bookquestions@oreilly.com

For more information about our books, courses, conferences, and news, see our website at *http://www.oreilly.com*.

Find us on Facebook: *http://facebook.com/oreilly*

Follow us on Twitter: *http://twitter.com/oreillymedia*

Watch us on YouTube: *http://www.youtube.com/oreillymedia*

CHAPTER 1

Complexity Science

What Is This Book About?

This book is about data structures and algorithms, intermediate programming in Python, computational modeling, and the philosophy of science.

Data structures and algorithms
A data structure is a collection of data elements organized in a way that supports particular operations. For example, a Python dictionary organizes key-value pairs in a way that provides fast mapping from keys to values, but mapping from values to keys is slower.

An algorithm is a mechanical process for performing a computation. Designing efficient programs often involves the co-evolution of data structures and the algorithms that use them. For example, in the first few chapters I present graphs, data structures that implement graphs, and graph algorithms based on those data structures.

Python programming
This book picks up where *Think Python* leaves off. I assume that you have read that book or have equivalent knowledge of Python. I try to emphasize fundamental ideas that apply to programming in many languages, but along the way you will learn some useful features that are specific to Python.

Computational modeling
A model is a simplified description of a system used for simulation or analysis. Computational models are designed to take advantage of cheap, fast computation.

Philosophy of science
The experiments and results in this book raise questions relevant to the philosophy of science, including the nature of scientific laws, theory choice, realism and instrumentalism, holism and reductionism, and epistemology.

This book is also about **complexity science**, which is an interdisciplinary field (at the intersection of mathematics, computer science, and natural science) that focuses on discrete models of physical systems. In particular, it focuses on **complex systems**, which are systems with many interacting components.

Complex systems include networks and graphs, cellular automata, agent-based models and swarms, fractals and self-organizing systems, chaotic systems, and cybernetic systems. These terms might not mean much to you at this point. We will get to them soon, but you can get a preview at *http://en.wikipedia.org/wiki/Complex_systems*.

A New Kind of Science

In 2002, Stephen Wolfram published *A New Kind of Science*, where he presents his and others' work on cellular automata and describes a scientific approach to the study of computational systems. We'll get back to Wolfram in Chapter 6, but I want to borrow his title for something a little broader.

I think complexity is a "new kind of science" not because it applies the tools of science to a new subject, but because it uses different tools, allows different kinds of work, and ultimately changes what we mean by "science."

To demonstrate the difference, I'll start with an example of classical science: suppose someone asked you why planetary orbits are elliptical. You might invoke Newton's law of universal gravitation and use it to write a differential equation that describes planetary motion. Then you could solve the differential equation and show that the solution is an ellipse. Voilà!

Most people find this kind of explanation satisfying. It includes a mathematical derivation—so it has some of the rigor of a proof—and it explains a specific observation, elliptical orbits, by appealing to a general principle, gravitation.

Let me contrast that with a different kind of explanation. Suppose you move to a city like Detroit that is racially segregated, and you want to know why it's like that. If you do some research, you might find a paper by Thomas Schelling called "Dynamic Models of Segregation," which proposes a simple model of racial segregation (a copy is available from *http://statistics.berkeley.edu/~aldous/157/Papers/Schelling_Seg_Models.pdf*).

Here is a summary of the paper (from Chapter 10):

> The Schelling model of the city is an array of cells where each cell represents a house. The houses are occupied by two kinds of "agents," labeled red and blue, in roughly equal numbers. About 10% of the houses are empty.

> At any point in time, an agent might be happy or unhappy, depending on the other agents in the neighborhood. In one version of the model, agents are happy if they have at least two neighbors like themselves, and unhappy if they have one or zero.

> The simulation proceeds by choosing an agent at random and checking to see whether it is happy. If so, nothing happens; if not, the agent chooses one of the unoccupied cells at random and moves.

If you start with a simulated city that is entirely unsegregated and run the model for a short time, clusters of similar agents appear. As time passes, the clusters grow and coalesce until there are a small number of large clusters and most agents live in homogeneous neighborhoods.

The degree of segregation in the model is surprising, and it suggests an explanation of segregation in real cities. Maybe Detroit is segregated because people prefer not to be greatly outnumbered and will move if the composition of their neighborhoods makes them unhappy.

Is this explanation satisfying in the same way as the explanation of planetary motion? Most people would say not, but why?

Most obviously, the Schelling model is highly abstract, which is to say it is not realistic. It is tempting to say that people are more complex than planets, but when you think about it, planets are just as complex as people (especially the ones that *have* people).

Both systems are complex, and both models are based on simplifications; for example, in the model of planetary motion, we include forces between the planet and its sun and ignore interactions between planets.

The important difference is that, for planetary motion, we can defend the model by showing that the forces we ignore are smaller than the ones we include. And we can extend the model to include other interactions and show that the effect is small. For Schelling's model, it is harder to justify the simplifications.

To make matters worse, Schelling's model doesn't appeal to any physical laws, and it uses only simple computation, not mathematical derivation. Models like Schelling's don't look like classical science, and many people find them less compelling, at least at first. But as I will try to demonstrate, these models do useful work, including prediction, explanation, and design. One of the goals of this book is to explain how.

Paradigm Shift?

When I describe this book to people, I am often asked if this new kind of science is a paradigm shift. I don't think so, and here's why.

Thomas Kuhn introduced the term "paradigm shift" in *The Structure of Scientific Revolutions* in 1962. It refers to a process in the history of science where the basic assumptions of a field change, or where one theory is replaced by another. He presents as examples the Copernican revolution, the displacement of phlogiston by the oxygen model of combustion, and the emergence of relativity.

The development of complexity science is not the replacement of an older model, but (in my opinion) a gradual shift in the criteria by which models are judged and in the kinds of models that are considered acceptable.

For example, classical models tend to be law-based, expressed in the form of equations, and solved by mathematical derivation. Models that fall under the umbrella of complexity are often rule-based, expressed as computations, and simulated rather than analyzed.

Not everyone finds these models satisfactory. For example, in *Sync*, Steven Strogatz writes about his model of spontaneous synchronization in some species of fireflies. He presents a simulation that demonstrates the phenomenon, but then writes:

> I repeated the simulation dozens of times, for other random initial conditions and for other numbers of oscillators. Sync every time. ... The challenge now was to prove it. Only an ironclad proof would demonstrate, in a way that no computer ever could, that sync was inevitable; and the best kind of proof would clarify *why* it was inevitable.

Strogatz is a mathematician, so his enthusiasm for proofs is understandable, but his proof doesn't address what is, to me, the most interesting part of the phenomenon. In order to prove that "sync was inevitable," Strogatz makes several simplifying assumptions, in particular that each firefly can see all the others.

In my opinion, it is more interesting to explain how an entire valley of fireflies can synchronize *despite the fact that they cannot all see each other*. How this kind of global behavior emerges from local interactions is the subject of Chapter 10. Explanations of these phenomena often use agent-based models, which explore (in ways that would be difficult or impossible with mathematical analysis) the conditions that allow or prevent synchronization.

I am a computer scientist, so my enthusiasm for computational models is probably no surprise. I don't mean to say that Strogatz is wrong, but rather that people disagree about what questions to ask and what tools to use to answer them. These decisions are based on value judgments, so there is no reason to expect agreement.

Nevertheless, there is rough consensus among scientists about which models are considered good science and which others are fringe science, pseudoscience, or not science at all.

I claim—and this is a central thesis of this book—that the criteria upon which this consensus is based change over time, and that the emergence of complexity science reflects a gradual shift in these criteria.

The Axes of Scientific Models

I have described classical models as based on physical laws, expressed in the form of equations, and solved by mathematical analysis; conversely, models of complexity systems are often based on simple rules and implemented as computations.

We can think of this trend as a shift over time along two axes:

Equation-based → *simulation-based*
Analysis → *computation*

The new kind of science is different in several other ways. I present them here so you know what's coming, but some of them might not make sense until you have seen the examples later in the book.

Continuous → *discrete*
Classical models tend to be based on continuous mathematics like calculus; models of complex systems are often based on discrete mathematics, including graphs and cellular automata.

Linear → *non-linear*
Classical models are often linear or use linear approximations to non-linear systems; complexity science is more friendly to non-linear models. One example is chaos theory.[1]

Deterministic → *stochastic*
Classical models are usually deterministic, which may reflect underlying philosophical determinism, discussed in Chapter 6; complex models often feature randomness.

Abstract → *detailed*
In classical models, planets are point masses, planes are frictionless, and cows are spherical (see *http://en.wikipedia.org/wiki/Spherical_cow*). Simplifications like these are often necessary for analysis, but computational models can be more realistic.

One, two → *many*
In celestial mechanics, the two-body problem can be solved analytically; the three-body problem cannot. Where classical models are often limited to small numbers of interacting elements, complexity science works with larger complexes (which is where the name comes from).

Homogeneous → *composite*
In classical models, the elements tend to be interchangeable; complex models more often include heterogeneity.

These are generalizations, so we should not take them too seriously. And I don't mean to deprecate classical science. A more complicated model is not necessarily better; in fact, it is usually worse.

Also, I don't mean to say that these changes are abrupt or complete. Rather, there is a gradual migration in the frontier of what is considered acceptable, respectable work. Some tools that used to be regarded with suspicion are now common, and some models that were widely accepted are now regarded with scrutiny.

---

1. Chaos is not covered in this book, but you can read about it at *http://en.wikipedia.org/wiki/Chaos_theory*.

For example, when Appel and Haken proved the four-color theorem in 1976, they used a computer to enumerate 1,936 special cases that were, in some sense, lemmas of their proof. At the time, many mathematicians did not consider the theorem truly proved. Now, computer-assisted proofs are common and generally (but not universally) accepted.

Conversely, a substantial body of economic analysis is based on a model of human behavior called "economic man," or, with tongue in cheek, *Homo economicus*. Research based on this model was highly regarded for several decades, especially if it involved mathematical virtuosity. More recently, this model is treated with more skepticism, and models that include imperfect information and bounded rationality are hot topics.

A New Kind of Model

Complex models are often appropriate for different purposes and interpretations.

Predictive → explanatory
> Schelling's model of segregation might shed light on a complex social phenomenon, but it is not useful for prediction. On the other hand, a simple model of celestial mechanics can predict solar eclipses down to the second, years in the future.

Realism → instrumentalism
> Classical models lend themselves to a realist interpretation; for example, most people accept that electrons are real things that exist. Instrumentalism is the view that models can be useful even if the entities they postulate don't exist. George Box wrote what might be the motto of instrumentalism: "All models are wrong, but some are useful."

Reductionism → holism
> Reductionism is the view that the behavior of a system can be explained by understanding its components. For example, the periodic table of the elements is a triumph of reductionism, because it explains the chemical behavior of elements with a simple model of the electrons in an atom. Holism is the view that some phenomena that appear at the system level do not exist at the level of components, and cannot be explained in component-level terms.

We get back to explanatory models in Chapter 5, instrumentalism in Chapter 7, and holism in Chapter 9.

A New Kind of Engineering

I have been talking about complex systems in the context of science, but complexity is also a cause, and effect, of changes in engineering and the organization of social systems.

Centralized → decentralized

> Centralized systems are conceptually simple and easier to analyze, but decentralized systems can be more robust. For example, on the World Wide Web, clients send requests to centralized servers; if the servers are down, the service is unavailable. In peer-to-peer networks, every node is both a client and a server. To take down the service, you have to take down *every* node.

Isolation → interaction

> In classical engineering, the complexity of large systems is managed by isolating components and minimizing interactions. This is still an important engineering principle; nevertheless, the availability of cheap computation makes it increasingly feasible to design systems with complex interactions between components.

One-to-many → many-to-many

> In many communication systems, broadcast services are being augmented (and sometimes replaced) by services that allow users to communicate with each other and create, share, and modify content.

Top-down → bottom-up

> In social, political, and economic systems, many activities that would normally be centrally organized now operate as grassroots movements. Even armies, which are the canonical example of hierarchical structure, are moving toward devolved command and control.

Analysis → computation

> In classical engineering, the space of feasible designs is limited by our capability for analysis. For example, designing the Eiffel Tower was possible because Gustave Eiffel developed novel analytic techniques, in particular for dealing with wind load. Now tools for computer-aided design and analysis make it possible to build almost anything that can be imagined. Frank Gehry's Guggenheim Museum Bilbao is my favorite example.

Design → search

> Engineering is sometimes described as a search for solutions in a landscape of possible designs. Increasingly, the search process can be automated. For example, genetic algorithms explore large design spaces and discover solutions human engineers would not imagine (or like). The ultimate genetic algorithm, evolution, notoriously generates designs that violate the rules of human engineering.

A New Kind of Thinking

We are getting farther afield now, but the shifts I am postulating in the criteria of scientific modeling are related to 20th-century developments in logic and epistemology.

Aristotelian logic → many-valued logic

In traditional logic, any proposition is either true or false. This system lends itself to math-like proofs, but fails (in dramatic ways) for many real-world applications. Alternatives include many-valued logic, fuzzy logic, and other systems designed to handle indeterminacy, vagueness, and uncertainty. Bart Kosko discusses some of these systems in *Fuzzy Thinking*.

Frequentist probability → Bayesianism

Bayesian probability has been around for centuries but was not widely used until recently, facilitated by the availability of cheap computation and the reluctant acceptance of subjectivity in probabilistic claims. Sharon Bertsch McGrayne presents this history in *The Theory That Would Not Die*.

Objective → subjective

The Enlightenment and philosophic modernism are based on a belief in objective truth; that is, truths that are independent of the people who hold them. 20th-century developments including quantum mechanics, Gödel's Incompleteness Theorem, and Kuhn's study of the history of science called attention to seemingly unavoidable subjectivity in even "hard sciences" and mathematics. Rebecca Goldstein presents the historical context of Gödel's proof in *Incompleteness*.

Physical law → theory → model

Some people distinguish between laws, theories, and models, but I think they are the same thing. People who use "law" are likely to believe that it is objectively true and immutable, people who use "theory" concede that it is subject to revision, and people who use "model" concede that it is based on simplification and approximation.

Some concepts that are called "physical laws" are really definitions; others are, in effect, the assertion that a model predicts or explains the behavior of a system particularly well. We come back to the nature of physical models in the sections "Explanatory Models" on page 54 and "Reductionism and Holism" on page 92.

Determinism → indeterminism

Determinism is the view that all events are inevitably caused by prior events. Forms of indeterminism include randomness, probabilistic causation, and fundamental uncertainty. We come back to this topic in the sections "Determinism" on page 64 and "Free Will" on page 104.

These trends are not universal or complete, but the center of opinion is shifting along these axes. As evidence, consider the reaction to Thomas Kuhn's *The Structure of Scientific Revolutions*, which was reviled when it was published and is now considered almost uncontroversial.

These trends are both cause and effect of complexity science. For example, highly abstracted models are more acceptable now because of the diminished expectation that there should be a unique, correct model for every system. Conversely, developments in complex systems challenge determinism and the related concept of physical law.

This chapter is an overview of the themes coming up in the book, but not all of it will make sense before you see the examples. When you get to the end of the book, you might find it helpful to read this chapter again.

CHAPTER 2

Graphs

What's a Graph?

To most people, a graph is a visual representation of a data set, like a bar chart or an EKG. That's not what this chapter is about.

In this chapter, a **graph** is an abstraction used to model a system that contains discrete, interconnected elements. The elements are represented by **nodes** (also called **vertices**), and the interconnections are represented by **edges**.

For example, you could represent a road map with one node for each city and one edge for each road between cities; or you could represent a social network using one node for each person, with an edge between two people if they are "friends" and no edge otherwise.

In some graphs, edges have different lengths (sometimes called "weights" or "costs"). For example, in a road map, the length of an edge might represent the distance between two cities, the travel time, or the bus fare. In a social network, there might be different kinds of edges to represent different kinds of relationships: friends, business associates, and so on.

Edges may be **undirected**, if they represent a relationship that is symmetric, or **directed**. In a social network, friendship is usually symmetric: if *A* is friends with *B*, then *B* is friends with *A*. So you would probably represent friendship with an undirected edge. In a road map, you would probably represent a one-way street with a directed edge.

Graphs have interesting mathematical properties, and there is a branch of mathematics called **graph theory** that studies them.

Graphs are also useful because there are many real-world problems that can be solved using **graph algorithms**. For example, Dijkstra's shortest path algorithm is an efficient way to find the shortest path from a node to all other nodes in a graph. (A **path** is a sequence of nodes with an edge between each consecutive pair.)

Sometimes the connection between a real-world problem and a graph algorithm is obvious. In the road map example, it is not hard to imagine using a shortest path algorithm to find the route between two cities that minimizes distance (or time, or cost).

In other cases, it takes more effort to represent a problem in a form that can be solved with a graph algorithm and then interpret the solution.

For example, a complex system of radioactive decay can be represented by a graph with one node for each nuclide (type of atom) and an edge between two nuclides if one can decay into the other. A path in this graph represents a decay chain. For more information, see *http://en.wikipedia.org/wiki/Radioactive_decay*.

The rate of decay between two nuclides is characterized by a decay constant, λ, measured in becquerels (Bq) or decay events per second. You might be more familiar with half-life, $t_{1/2}$, which is the expected time until half of a sample decays. You can convert from one characterization to the other using the relation $t_{1/2} = \ln 2/\lambda$.

In our best current model of physics, nuclear decay is a fundamentally random process, so it is impossible to predict when an atom will decay. However, given λ, the probability that an atom decays during a short time interval, dt, is λdt.

In a graph with multiple decay chains, the probability of a given path is the product of the probabilities of each decay process in the path.

Now suppose you want to find the decay chain with the highest probability. You could do it by assigning each edge a "length" of $-\log \lambda$ and using a shortest path algorithm. Why? Because the shortest path algorithm adds up the lengths of the edges, and adding up log probabilities is the same as multiplying probabilities. Also, because the logarithms are negated, the smallest sum corresponds to the largest probability. So the shortest path corresponds to the most likely decay chain.

This is an example of a common and useful process in applying graph algorithms:

1. *Reduce* a real-world problem to an instance of a graph problem.
2. *Apply* a graph algorithm to compute the result efficiently.
3. *Interpret* the result of the computation in terms of a solution to the original problem.

We will see other examples of this process soon.

Exercise 2-1.

Read the Wikipedia page about graphs at *http://en.wikipedia.org/wiki/Graph_(mathe matics)* and answer the following questions:

1. What is a simple graph? In the rest of this section, we will be assuming that all graphs are simple graphs. This is a common assumption for many graph algorithms —so common it is often unstated.
2. What is a regular graph? What is a complete graph? Prove that a complete graph is regular.
3. What is a path? What is a cycle?
4. What is a forest? What is a tree? Note: a graph is **connected** if there is a path from every node to every other node.

Representing Graphs

Graphs are usually drawn with squares or circles for nodes and lines for edges. In Figure 2-1, the graph on the left represents a social network with three people.

In the graph on the right, the weights of the edges are the approximate travel times (in hours) between cities in the northeast United States. In this case, the placement of the nodes corresponds roughly to the geography of the cities, but in general the layout of a graph is arbitrary.

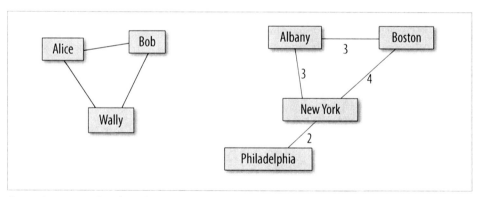

Figure 2-1. Examples of graphs

To implement graph algorithms, you have to figure out how to represent a graph in the form of a data structure. But to choose the best data structure, you have to know which operations the graph should support.

To get out of this chicken-and-egg problem, I will present a data structure that is a good choice for many graph algorithms. Later we come back and evaluate its pros and cons.

Here is an implementation of a graph as a dictionary of dictionaries:

```python
class Graph(dict):
    def __init__(self, vs=[], es=[]):
        """create a new graph.  (vs) is a list of vertices;
        (es) is a list of edges."""
        for v in vs:
            self.add_vertex(v)

        for e in es:
            self.add_edge(e)

    def add_vertex(self, v):
        """add (v) to the graph"""
        self[v] = {}

    def add_edge(self, e):
        """add (e) to the graph by adding an entry in both directions.

        If there is already an edge connecting these Vertices, the
        new edge replaces it.
        """
        v, w = e
        self[v][w] = e
        self[w][v] = e
```

The first line declares that Graph inherits from the built-in type dict, so a Graph object has all the methods and operators of a dictionary.

More specifically, a Graph is a dictionary that maps from a Vertex v to an inner dictionary that maps from a Vertex w to an Edge that connects v and w. So if g is a graph, g[v][w] maps to an Edge if there is one, and raises a KeyError otherwise.

__init__ takes a list of vertices and a list of edges as optional parameters. If they are provided, it calls add_vertex and add_edge to add the vertices and edges to the graph.

Adding a vertex to a graph means making an entry for it in the outer dictionary. Adding an edge makes two entries, both pointing to the same Edge, so this implementation represents an undirected graph.

Here is the definition for Vertex:

```python
class Vertex(object):
    def __init__(self, label=''):
        self.label = label

    def __repr__(self):
        return 'Vertex(%s)' % repr(self.label)

    __str__ = __repr__
```

A Vertex is just an object that has a label attribute. We can add attributes later as needed.

__repr__ is a special function that returns a string representation of an object. It is similar to __str__ except that the return value from __str__ is intended to be readable for people, and the return value from __repr__ is supposed to be a legal Python expression.

The built-in function str invokes __str__ on an object; similarly, the built-in function repr invokes __repr__.

In this case, Vertex.__str__ and Vertex.__repr__ refer to the same function, so we get the same string either way.

Here is the definition for Edge:

```
class Edge(tuple):
    def __new__(cls, e1, e2):
        return tuple.__new__(cls, (e1, e2))

    def __repr__(self):
        return 'Edge(%s, %s)' % (repr(self[0]), repr(self[1]))

    __str__ = __repr__
```

Edge inherits from the built-in type tuple and overrides the __new__ method. When you invoke an object constructor, Python invokes __new__ to create the object and then __init__ to initialize the attributes.

For mutable objects, it is most common to override __init__ and use the default implementation of __new__, but because edges inherit from tuple, they are immutable, which means that you can't modify the elements of the tuple in __init__. By overriding __new__, we can use the parameters to initialize the elements of the tuple.

Here is an example that creates two vertices and an edge:

```
v = Vertex('v')
w = Vertex('w')
e = Edge(v, w)
print e
```

Inside Edge.__str__, the term self[0] refers to v and self[1] refers to w, so the output when you print e is:

```
Edge(Vertex('v'), Vertex('w'))
```

Now we can assemble the edge and vertices into a graph:

```
g = Graph([v, w], [e])
print g
```

The output looks like this (with a little formatting):

```
{Vertex('w'): {Vertex('v'): Edge(Vertex('v'), Vertex('w'))},
 Vertex('v'): {Vertex('w'): Edge(Vertex('v'), Vertex('w'))}}
```

We didn't have to write Graph.__str__; it is inherited from dict.

Exercise 2-2.

In this exercise, you will write methods that will be useful for many of the graph algorithms that are coming up.

1. Download *http://thinkcomplex.com/GraphCode.py*, which contains the code in this chapter. Run it as a script, and make sure the test code in main does what you expect.

2. Make a copy of GraphCode.py called Graph.py. Add the methods in Steps 3-9 to Graph, adding test code as you go.

3. Write a method named get_edge that takes two vertices and returns the edge between them if it exists and None otherwise. Hint: use a try statement.

4. Write a method named remove_edge that takes an edge and removes all references to it from the graph.

5. Write a method named vertices that returns a list of the vertices in a graph.

6. Write a method named edges that returns a list of edges in a graph. Note that in our representation of an undirected graph, there are two references to each edge.

7. Write a method named out_vertices that takes a Vertex and returns a list of the adjacent vertices (the ones connected to the given node by an edge).

8. Write a method named out_edges that takes a Vertex and returns a list of edges connected to the given Vertex.

9. Write a method named add_all_edges that starts with an edgeless Graph and makes a complete graph by adding edges between all pairs of vertices.

Test your methods by writing test code and checking the output. Then download *http://thinkcomplex.com/GraphWorld.py*. GraphWorld is a simple tool for generating visual representations of graphs. It is based on the World class in Swampy, so you might have to install Swampy first: see *http://thinkpython.com/swampy*.

Read through GraphWorld.py to get a sense of how it works. Then run it. It should import your Graph.py and then display a complete graph with 10 vertices.

Exercise 2-3.

Write a method named add_regular_edges that starts with an edgeless graph and adds edges so that every vertex has the same degree. The **degree** of a node is the number of edges it is connected to.

To create a regular graph with degree 2, you would do something like this:

```
vertices = [ ... list of Vertices ... ]
g = Graph(vertices, [])
g.add_regular_edges(2)
```

It is not always possible to create a regular graph with a given degree, so you should figure out and document the preconditions for this method.

To test your code, you might want to create a file named GraphTest.py that imports Graph.py and GraphWorld.py, then generates and displays the graphs you want to test.

Random Graphs

A random graph is just what it sounds like: a graph with edges generated at random. Of course, there are many random processes that can generate graphs, so there are many kinds of random graphs. One interesting kind is the Erdős-Rényi model, denoted $G(n, p)$, which generates graphs with n nodes, where the probability is p that there is an edge between any two nodes. See *http://en.wikipedia.org/wiki/Erdos-Renyi_model*.

Exercise 2-4.

Create a file named RandomGraph.py, and define a class named RandomGraph that inherits from Graph and provides a method named add_random_edges that takes a probability p as a parameter and, starting with an edgeless graph, adds edges at random so that the probability is p that there is an edge between any two nodes.

Connected Graphs

A graph is **connected** if there is a path from every node to every other node. See *http://en.wikipedia.org/wiki/Connectivity_(graph_theory)*.

There is a simple algorithm to check whether a graph is connected. Start at any vertex and conduct a search (usually a breadth-first-search or BFS), marking all the vertices you can reach. Then check to see whether all vertices are marked.

You can read about breadth-first-search at *http://en.wikipedia.org/wiki/Breadth-first _search*.

In general, when you process a node, we say that you are **visiting** it.

In a search, you visit a node by marking it (so you can tell later that it has been visited), then visiting any unmarked vertices it is connected to.

In a breadth-first-search, you visit nodes in the order they are discovered. You can use a queue or a "worklist" to keep them in order. Here's how it works:

1. Start with any vertex and add it to the queue.
2. Remove a vertex from the queue and mark it. If it is connected to any unmarked vertices, add them to the queue.
3. If the queue is not empty, go back to Step 2.

Exercise 2-5.

Write a Graph method named is_connected that returns True if the Graph is connected and False otherwise.

Paul Erdős: Peripatetic Mathematician, Speed Freak

Paul Erdős was a Hungarian mathematician who spent most of his career (from 1934 until his death in 1992) living out of a suitcase, visiting colleagues at universities all over the world, and authoring papers with more than 500 collaborators.

He was a notorious caffeine addict and, for the last 20 years of his life, an enthusiastic user of amphetamines. He attributed at least some of his productivity to the use of these drugs; after giving them up for a month to win a bet, he complained that the only result was that mathematics had been set back by a month.[1]

In the 1960s, he and Alfréd Rényi wrote a series of papers introducing the Erdős-Rényi model of random graphs and studying their properties. The second paper is available from *http://www.renyi.hu/~p_erdos/1960-10.pdf*.

One of their most surprising results is the existence of abrupt changes in the characteristics of random graphs as random edges are added. They showed that for a number of graph properties, there is a threshold value of the probability p below which the property is rare and above which it is almost certain. This transition is sometimes called a "phase change" as an analogy with physical systems that change state at some critical value of temperature. See *http://en.wikipedia.org/wiki/Phase_transition*.

Exercise 2-6.

One of the properties that displays this kind of transition is connectedness. For a given size n, there is a critical value, $p*$, such that a random graph $G(n, p)$ is unlikely to be connected if $p < p*$ and very likely to be connected if $p > p*$.

Write a program that tests this result by generating random graphs for values of n and p, and then computing the fraction of the values that are connected.

How does the abruptness of the transition depend on n?

You can download my solution from *http://thinkcomplex.com/RandomGraph.py*.

Iterators

If you have read the documentation of Python dictionaries, you might have noticed the methods `iterkeys`, `itervalues`, and `iteritems`. These methods are similar to `keys`, `values`, and `items` except that instead of building a new list, they return iterators.

An **iterator** is an object that provides a method named `next` that returns the next element in a sequence. Here is an example that creates a dictionary and uses `iterkeys` to traverse the keys.

---

1. Much of this biography follows *http://en.wikipedia.org/wiki/Paul_Erdos*.

```
>>> d = dict(a=1, b=2)
>>> iter = d.iterkeys()
>>> print iter.next()
a
>>> print iter.next()
b
>>> print iter.next()
Traceback (most recent call last):
  File "<stdin>", line 1, in <module>
StopIteration
```

The first time next is invoked, it returns the first key from the dictionary (the order of the keys is arbitrary). The second time it is invoked, it returns the second element. The third time, and every time thereafter, it raises a StopIteration exception.

An iterator can be used in a for loop; for example, the following is a common idiom for traversing the key-value pairs in a dictionary:

```
for k, v in d.iteritems():
        print k, v
```

In this context, iteritems is likely to be faster than items because it doesn't have to build the entire list of tuples; it reads them from the dictionary as it goes along.

But it is only safe to use the iterator methods if you do not add or remove dictionary keys inside the loop. Otherwise you get an exception:

```
>>> d = dict(a=1)
>>> for k in d.iterkeys():
...        d['b'] = 2
...
RuntimeError: dictionary changed size during iteration
```

Another limitation of iterators is that they do not support index operations:

```
>>> iter = d.iterkeys()
>>> print iter[1]
TypeError: 'dictionary-keyiterator' object is unsubscriptable
```

If you need indexed access, you should use keys. Alternatively, the Python module itertools provides many useful iterator functions.

A user-defined object can be used as an iterator if it provides methods named next and __iter__. The following example is an iterator that always returns True:

```
class AllTrue(object):
    def next(self):
        return True

    def __iter__(self):
        return self
```

The __iter__ method for iterators returns the iterator itself. This protocol makes it possible to use iterators and sequences interchangeably in many contexts.

Iterators like `AllTrue` can represent an infinite sequence. They are useful as an argument to `zip`:

```
>>> print zip('abc', AllTrue())
[('a', True), ('b', True), ('c', True)]
```

Generators

For many purposes, the easiest way to make an iterator is to write a **generator**, which is a function that contains a `yield` statement. `yield` is similar to `return`, except that the state of the running function is stored and can be resumed.

For example, here is a generator that yields successive letters of the alphabet:

```
def generate_letters():
    for letter in 'abc':
        yield letter
```

When you call this function, the return value is an iterator:

```
>>> iter = generate_letters()
>>> print iter
<generator object at 0xb7d4ce4c>
>>> print iter.next()
a
>>> print iter.next()
b
```

And you can use an iterator in a `for` loop:

```
>>> for letter in generate_letters():
...     print letter
...
a
b
c
```

A generator with an infinite loop returns an iterator that never terminates. For example, here's a generator that cycles through the letters of the alphabet:

```
def alphabet_cycle():
    while True:
        for c in string.lowercase:
            yield c
```

Exercise 2-7.

Write a generator that yields an infinite sequence of alphanumeric identifiers, starting with `a1` through `z1`, then `a2` through `z2`, and so on.

CHAPTER 3

Analysis of Algorithms

Analysis of algorithms is the branch of computer science that studies the performance of algorithms, especially their runtime and space requirements. For more information, see *http://en.wikipedia.org/wiki/Analysis_of_algorithms*.

The practical goal of algorithm analysis is to predict the performance of different algorithms in order to guide design decisions.

During the 2008 United States presidential campaign, candidate Barack Obama was asked to perform an impromptu analysis when he visited Google. Chief executive Eric Schmidt jokingly asked him for "the most efficient way to sort a million 32-bit integers." Obama had apparently been tipped off, because he quickly replied, "I think the bubble sort would be the wrong way to go." See *http://www.youtube.com/watch?v=k4RRi _ntQc8*.

This is true: bubble sort is conceptually simple but slow for large datasets. The answer Schmidt was probably looking for is "radix sort" (see *http://en.wikipedia.org/wiki/Radix _sort*).[1]

The goal of algorithm analysis is to make meaningful comparisons between algorithms, but there are some problems:

- The relative performance of the algorithms might depend on characteristics of the hardware, so one algorithm might be faster on Machine A, another on Machine B. The general solution to this problem is to specify a **machine model** and analyze the number of steps (or operations) an algorithm requires under a given model.

1. But if you get a question like this in an interview, I think a better answer is, "The fastest way to sort a million integers is to use whatever sort function is provided by the language I'm using. Its performance is good enough for the vast majority of applications, but if it turned out that my application was too slow, I would use a profiler to see where the time was being spent. If it looked like a faster sort algorithm would have a significant effect on performance, then I would look around for a good implementation of radix sort."

- Relative performance might depend on the details of the dataset. For example, some sorting algorithms run faster if the data are already partially sorted; other algorithms run slower in this case. A common way to avoid this problem is to analyze the *worst case* scenario. It is also sometimes useful to analyze average case performance, but it is usually harder, and sometimes it is not clear what set of cases to average.
- Relative performance also depends on the size of the problem. A sorting algorithm that is fast for small lists might be slow for long lists. The usual solution to this problem is to express runtime (or number of operations) as a function of problem size and to compare the functions *asymptotically* as the problem size increases.

The good thing about this kind of comparison is that it lends itself to simple classification of algorithms. For example, if I know that the runtime of Algorithm A tends to be proportional to the size of the input n, and Algorithm B tends to be proportional to n^2, then I expect A to be faster than B for large values of n.

This kind of analysis comes with some caveats, but we'll get to that later.

Order of Growth

Suppose you have analyzed two algorithms and expressed their runtimes in terms of the size of the input: Algorithm A takes $100n + 1$ steps to solve a problem with size n, and Algorithm B takes $n^2 + n + 1$ steps.

The following table shows the runtime of these algorithms for different problem sizes:

Input size	Runtime of Algorithm A	Runtime of Algorithm B
10	1 001	111
100	10 001	10 101
1 000	100 001	1 001 001
10 000	1 000 001	$> 10^{10}$

At $n = 10$, Algorithm A looks pretty bad; it takes almost 10 times longer than Algorithm B. But for $n = 100$, they are about the same, and for larger values, A is much better.

The fundamental reason is that for large values of n, any function that contains an n^2 term will grow faster than a function whose leading term is n. The **leading term** is the term with the highest exponent.

For Algorithm A, the leading term has a large coefficient, 100, which is why B does better than A for a small n. But regardless of the coefficients, there will always be some value of n where $an^2 > bn$.

The same argument applies to the non-leading terms. Even if the runtime of Algorithm A were $n + 1000000$, it would still be better than Algorithm B for a sufficiently large n.

In general, we expect an algorithm with a smaller leading term to be a better algorithm for large problems, but for smaller problems, there may be a **crossover point** where another algorithm is better. The location of the crossover point depends on the details of the algorithms, the inputs, and the hardware, so it is usually ignored for purposes of algorithmic analysis. But that doesn't mean you can forget about it.

If two algorithms have the same leading order term, it is hard to say which is better; again, the answer depends on the details. So for algorithmic analysis, functions with the same leading term are considered equivalent, even if they have different coefficients.

An **order of growth** is a set of functions whose asymptotic growth behavior is considered equivalent. For example, $2n$, $100n$, and $n + 1$ belong to the same order of growth, which is written $O(n)$ in **Big O notation**, and often called **linear** because every function in the set grows linearly with n.

All functions with the leading term n^2 belong to $O(n^2)$; they are **quadratic**, which is a fancy word for functions with the leading term n^2.

The following table shows some of the orders of growth that appear most commonly in algorithmic analysis, in increasing order of badness.

Order of growth	Name
$O(1)$	constant
$O(\log_b n)$	logarithmic (for any b)
$O(n)$	linear
$O(n \log_b n)$	"en log en"
$O(n^2)$	quadratic
$O(n^3)$	cubic
$O(c^n)$	exponential (for any c)

For the logarithmic terms, the base of the logarithm doesn't matter; changing bases is the equivalent of multiplying by a constant, which doesn't change the order of growth. Similarly, all exponential functions belong to the same order of growth regardless of the base of the exponent. Exponential functions grow very quickly, so exponential algorithms are only useful for small problems.

Exercise 3-1.

Read the Wikipedia page on Big O notation at *http://en.wikipedia.org/wiki/Big_O_notation*, and answer the following questions:

1. What is the order of growth of $n^3 + n^2$? What about $1000000n^3 + n^2$? What about $n^3 + 1000000n^2$?

2. What is the order of growth of $(n^2 + n) \cdot (n + 1)$? Before you start multiplying, remember that you only need the leading term.

3. If f is in $O(g)$ for some unspecified function g, what can we say about $af + b$?

4. If f_1 and f_2 are in $O(g)$, what can we say about $f_1 + f_2$?

5. If f_1 is in $O(g)$ and f_2 is in $O(h)$, what can we say about $f_1 + f_2$?

6. If f_1 is in $O(g)$ and f_2 is $O(h)$, what can we say about $f_1 * f_2$?

Programmers who care about performance often find this kind of analysis hard to swallow. They have a point: sometimes the coefficients and the non-leading terms make a real difference, and sometimes the details of the hardware, the programming language, and the characteristics of the input make a big difference. Also, for small problems, asymptotic behavior is irrelevant.

But if you keep those caveats in mind, algorithmic analysis is a useful tool. At least for large problems, the "better" algorithm is usually better, and sometimes it is *much* better. The difference between two algorithms with the same order of growth is usually a constant factor, but the difference between a good algorithm and a bad algorithm is unbounded!

Analysis of Basic Python Operations

Most arithmetic operations are constant time; multiplication usually takes longer than addition and subtraction, and division takes even longer, but these runtimes don't depend on the magnitude of the operands. Very large integers are an exception; in that case, the runtime increases with the number of digits.

Indexing operations—reading or writing elements in a sequence or dictionary—are also constant time, regardless of the size of the data structure.

A for loop that traverses a sequence or dictionary is usually linear, as long as all of the operations in the body of the loop are constant time. For example, adding up the elements of a list is linear:

```
total = 0
    for x in t:
        total += x
```

The built-in function sum is also linear because it does the same thing, but it tends to be faster because it is a more efficient implementation. In the language of algorithmic analysis, it has a smaller leading coefficient.

If you use the same loop to "add" a list of strings, the runtime is quadratic because string concatenation is linear. The string method join is usually faster because it is linear in the total length of the strings.

As a rule of thumb, if the body of a loop is in $O(n^a)$, then the whole loop is in $O(n^{a+1})$. The exception is if you can show that the loop exits after a constant number of iterations. If a loop runs k times regardless of n, then the loop is in $O(n^a)$, even for a large k.

Multiplying by k doesn't change the order of growth, but neither does dividing. So if the body of a loop is in $O(n^a)$ and it runs n / k times, the loop is in $O(n^{a+1})$, even for a large k.

Most string and tuple operations are linear, except indexing and `len`, which are constant time. The built-in functions `min` and `max` are linear. The runtime of a slice operation is proportional to the length of the output, but independent of the size of the input.

All string methods are linear, but if the lengths of the strings are bounded by a constant—for example, operations on single characters—they are considered constant time.

Most list methods are linear, but there are some exceptions:

- Adding an element to the end of a list is constant time on average. When it runs out of room, it occasionally gets copied to a bigger location, but the total time for n operations is $O(n)$, so we say that the "amortized" time for one operation is $O(1)$.
- Removing an element from the end of a list is constant time.
- Sorting is $O(n \log n)$.

Most dictionary operations and methods are constant time, but there are some exceptions:

- The runtime of `copy` is proportional to the number of elements, but not to the size of the elements (it copies references, not the elements themselves).
- The runtime of `update` is proportional to the size of the dictionary passed as a parameter, not the dictionary being updated.
- `keys`, `values`, and `items` are linear because they return new lists; `iterkeys`, `iter values`, and `iteritems` are constant time because they return iterators. But if you loop through the iterators, the loop will be linear. Using the "iter" functions saves some overhead, but it doesn't change the order of growth unless the number of items you access is bounded.

The performance of dictionaries is one of the minor miracles of computer science. We will see how they work in "Hashtables" on page 27.

Exercise 3-2.

Read the Wikipedia page on sorting algorithms at *http://en.wikipedia.org/wiki/Sorting _algorithm*, and answer the following questions:

1. What is a "comparison sort"? What is the best worst-case order of growth for a comparison sort? What is the best worst-case order of growth for any sort algorithm?
2. What is the order of growth of bubble sort, and why does Barack Obama think it is "the wrong way to go"?

3. What is the order of growth of radix sort? What preconditions do we need to use it?

4. What is a stable sort, and why might it matter in practice?

5. What is the worst sorting algorithm (that has a name)?

6. What sort algorithm does the C library use? What sort algorithm does Python use? Are these algorithms stable? (You might have to Google around to find these answers.)

7. Many of the non-comparison sorts are linear, so why does Python use an $O(n \log n)$ comparison sort?

Analysis of Search Algorithms

A **search** is an algorithm that takes a collection and a target item and determines whether the target is in the collection, often returning the index of the target.

The simplest search algorithm is a "linear search," which traverses the items of the collection in order, stopping if it finds the target. In the worst case, it has to traverse the entire collection, so the runtime is linear.

The in operator for sequences uses a linear search; so do string methods like find and count.

If the elements of the sequence are in order, you can use a **bisection search**, which is $O(\log n)$. Bisection search is similar to the algorithm you probably use to look a word up in a dictionary (a real dictionary, not the data structure). Instead of starting at the beginning and checking each item in order, you start with the item in the middle and check whether the word you are looking for comes before or after. If it comes before, then you search the first half of the sequence. Otherwise, you search the second half. Either way, you cut the number of remaining items in half.

If the sequence has 1,000,000 items, it will take about 20 steps to find the word or conclude that it's not there. So that's about 50,000 times faster than a linear search.

Exercise 3-3.

Write a function called bisection that takes a sorted list and a target value and returns the index of the value in the list if it's there, or None if it's not.

You could also read the documentation of the bisect module and use that!

Bisection search can be much faster than linear search, but it requires the sequence to be in order, which might require extra work.

There is another data structure called a **hashtable** that is even faster—it can do a search in constant time, and doesn't require the items to be sorted. Python dictionaries are implemented using hashtables, which is why most dictionary operations, including the in operator, are constant time.

Hashtables

To explain how hashtables work and why their performance is so good, I start with a simple implementation of a map and gradually improve it until it's a hashtable.

I use Python to demonstrate these implementations, but in real life you wouldn't write code like this in Python; you would just use a dictionary! So for the rest of this chapter, you have to imagine that dictionaries don't exist and you want to implement a data structure that maps from keys to values. The operations you have to implement are:

add(k, v):
> Add a new item that maps from key k to value v. With a Python dictionary, d, this operation is written d[k] = v.

get(target):
> Look up and return the value that corresponds to key target. With a Python dictionary, d, this operation is written d[target] or d.get(target).

For now, I assume that each key only appears once. The simplest implementation of this interface uses a list of tuples, where each tuple is a key-value pair:

```
class LinearMap(object):

    def __init__(self):
        self.items = []

    def add(self, k, v):
        self.items.append((k, v))

    def get(self, k):
        for key, val in self.items:
            if key == k:
                return val
        raise KeyError
```

add appends a key-value tuple to the list of items, which takes constant time.

get uses a for loop to search the list. If it finds the target key, it returns the corresponding value; otherwise, it raises a KeyError (so get is linear).

An alternative is to keep the list sorted by key. Then get could use a bisection search, which is $O(\log n)$. But inserting a new item in the middle of a list is linear, so this might not be the best option. There are other data structures (see *http://en.wikipedia.org/wiki/Red-black_tree*) that can implement add and get in log time, but that's still not as good as constant time, so let's move on.

One way to improve LinearMap is to break the list of key-value pairs into smaller lists. Here's an implementation called BetterMap, which is a list of 100 LinearMaps. As we'll see in a second, the order of growth for get is still linear, but BetterMap is a step on the path toward hashtables:

```
class BetterMap(object):

    def __init__(self, n=100):
        self.maps = []
        for i in range(n):
            self.maps.append(LinearMap())

    def find_map(self, k):
        index = hash(k) % len(self.maps)
        return self.maps[index]

    def add(self, k, v):
        m = self.find_map(k)
        m.add(k, v)

    def get(self, k):
        m = self.find_map(k)
        return m.get(k)
```

__init__ makes a list of n LinearMaps.

find_map is used by add and get to figure out which map to put the new item in, or which map to search.

find_map uses the built-in function hash, which takes almost any Python object and returns an integer. A limitation of this implementation is that it only works with hashable keys. Mutable types like lists and dictionaries are unhashable.

Hashable objects that are considered equal return the same hash value, but the converse is not necessarily true: two different objects can return the same hash value.

find_map uses the modulus operator to wrap the hash values into the range from 0 to len(self.maps), so the result is a legal index into the list. Of course, this means that many different hash values will wrap onto the same index. But if the hash function spreads things out pretty evenly (which is what hash functions are designed to do), then we expect $n / 100$ items per LinearMap.

Since the runtime of LinearMap.get is proportional to the number of items, we expect BetterMap to be about 100 times faster than LinearMap. The order of growth is still linear, but the leading coefficient is smaller. That's nice, but still not as good as a hashtable.

Here (finally) is the crucial idea that makes hashtables fast: if you can keep the maximum length of the LinearMaps bounded, LinearMap.get is constant time. All you have to do is keep track of the number of items, and when the number of items per Linear Map exceeds a threshold, resize the hashtable by adding more LinearMaps.

Here is an implementation of a hashtable:

```
class HashMap(object):

    def __init__(self):
        self.maps = BetterMap(2)
        self.num = 0
```

```
def get(self, k):
    return self.maps.get(k)

def add(self, k, v):
    if self.num == len(self.maps.maps):
        self.resize()

    self.maps.add(k, v)
    self.num += 1

def resize(self):
    new_maps = BetterMap(self.num * 2)

    for m in self.maps.maps:
        for k, v in m.items:
            new_maps.add(k, v)

    self.maps = new_maps
```

Each HashMap contains a BetterMap. __init__ starts with just two LinearMaps and initializes num, which keeps track of the number of items.

get just dispatches to BetterMap. The real work happens in add, which checks the number of items and the size of the BetterMap: if they are equal, the average number of items per LinearMap is 1, so it calls resize.

resize makes a new BetterMap, twice as big as the previous one, and then "rehashes" the items from the old map to the new.

Rehashing is necessary because changing the number of LinearMaps changes the denominator of the modulus operator in find_map. That means that some objects that used to wrap into the same LinearMap will get split up—which is what we wanted, right?

Rehashing is linear, so resize is linear, which might seem bad since I promised that add would be constant time. But remember that we don't have to resize every time, so add is usually constant time and only occasionally linear. The total amount of work to run add n times is proportional to n, so the average time of each add is constant time!

To see how this works, think about starting with an empty hashtable and adding a sequence of items. We start with two LinearMaps, so the first two adds are fast (no resizing required). Let's say that they take one unit of work each. The next add requires a resize, so we have to rehash the first two items (let's call that two more units of work) and then add the third item (one more unit). Adding the next item costs one unit, so the total so far is six units of work for four items.

The next add costs 5 units, but the next three are only 1 unit each, so the total is 14 units for the first 8 adds.

The next add costs 9 units, but then we can add 7 more before the next resize, so the total is 30 units for the first 16 adds.

After 32 adds, the total cost is 62 units, and I hope you are starting to see a pattern. After *n* adds, where *n* is a power of two, the total cost is $2n - 2$ units, so the average work per add is a little less than two units. When *n* is a power of two, that's the best case; for other values of *n*, the average work is a little higher, but that's not important. The important thing is that it is $O(1)$.

Figure 3-1 shows how this works graphically. Each block represents a unit of work. The columns show the total work for each add in order from left to right; the first two adds cost one unit, the third costs three units, etc.

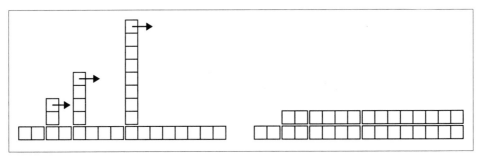

Figure 3-1. The cost of a hashtable add

The extra work of rehashing appears as a sequence of increasingly tall towers with increasing space between them. Now if you knock over the towers, amortizing the cost of resizing over all adds, you can see graphically that the total cost after *n* adds is $2n - 2$.

An important feature of this algorithm is that when we resize the hashtable, it grows geometrically; that is, we multiply the size by a constant. If you increase the size arithmetically—adding a fixed number each time—the average time per add is linear.

You can download my implementation of HashMap from *http://thinkcomplex.com/Map.py*, but remember that there is no reason to use it; if you want a map, just use a Python dictionary.

Exercise 3-4.

My implementation of HashMap accesses the attributes of BetterMap directly, which shows poor object-oriented design.

1. The special method __len__ is invoked by the built-in function len. Write a __len__ method for BetterMap and use it in add.

2. Use a generator to write BetterMap.iteritems, and use it in resize.

Exercise 3-5.

A drawback of hashtables is that the elements have to be hashable, which usually means they have to be immutable. That's why, in Python, you can use tuples but not lists as keys in a dictionary. An alternative is to use a tree-based map.

Write an implementation of the map interface called `TreeMap` that uses a red-black tree to perform `add` and `get` in log time.

Summing Lists

Suppose you have a bunch of lists and you want to join them up into a single list. There are three ways you might do that in Python.

- You could use the `+=` operator:

```
total = []
for x in t:
    total += x
```

- You could use the `extend` method:

```
total = []
for x in t:
    total.extend(x)
```

- Or you could use the built-in function `sum`:

```
total = sum(t, [])
```

The second argument to `sum` is the initial value for the total.

Without knowing how `+=`, `extend`, and `sum` are implemented, it is hard to analyze their performance. For example, if `total += x` creates a new list every time, the loop is quadratic, but if it modifies `total`, it's linear.

To find out, we could read the source code, but as an exercise, let's see if we can figure it out by measuring runtimes.

A simple way to measure the runtime of a program is to use the function `times` in the `os` module, which returns a tuple of floats indicating the time your process has used (see the documentation for details). I use a function, `etime`, which returns the sum of "user time" and "system time" (which is usually what we care about for performance measurement):

```
import os

def etime():
    """See how much user and system time this process has used
    so far and return the sum."""

    user, sys, chuser, chsys, real = os.times()
    return user+sys
```

To measure the elapsed time of a function, you can call `etime` twice and compute the difference:

```
start = etime()

    # put the code you want to measure here
```

```
end = etime()
elapsed = end - start
```

Alternatively, if you use IPython, you can use the `timeit` command. See *http://ipython .scipy.org*.

If an algorithm is quadratic, we expect the runtime, t, as a function of input size, n, to look like this:

$$t = an^2 + bn + c$$

where a, b, and c are unknown coefficients. If you take the log of both sides, you get:

$$\log t \sim \log a + 2 \log n$$

For large values of n, the non-leading terms are insignificant and this approximation is pretty good. So if we plot t versus n on a log-log scale, we expect a straight line with slope 2.

Similarly, if the algorithm is linear, we expect a line with slope 1.

I wrote three functions that concatenate lists: `sum_plus` uses `+=`, `sum_extend` uses `list.extend`, and `sum_sum` uses `sum`. I timed them for a range of n and plotted the results on a log-log scale. Figures 3-2 and 3-3 show the results.

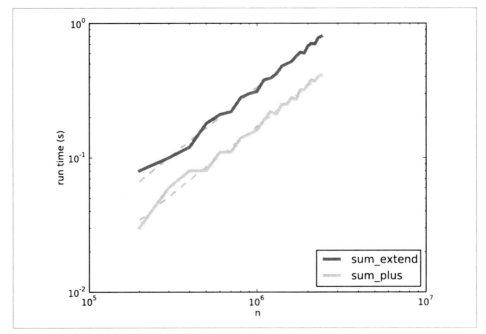

Figure 3-2. Runtime versus n (the dashed lines have slope 1)

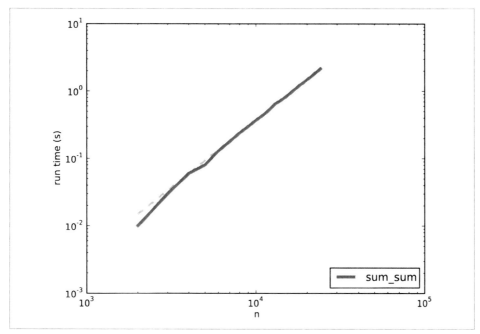

Figure 3-3. Runtime versus n (the dashed line has slope 2)

In Figure 3-2, I fit a line with slope 1 to the curves. The data fit this line well, so we conclude that these implementations are linear. The implementation for += is faster by a constant factor because it takes some time to look up the extend method each time through the loop.

In Figure 3-3, the data fit a line with slope 2, so the implementation of sum is quadratic.

pyplot

To make the figures in this section, I used pyplot, which is part of matplotlib. If matplotlib is not part of your Python installation, you might have to install it, or you can use another library to make plots.

Here's an example that makes a simple plot:

```
import matplotlib.pyplot as pyplot

pyplot.plot(xs, ys)
scale = 'log'
pyplot.xscale(scale)
pyplot.yscale(scale)
pyplot.title('')
pyplot.xlabel('n')
pyplot.ylabel('run time (s)')
pyplot.show()
```

The import statement makes `matplotlib.pyplot` accessible with the shorter name `pyplot`.

`plot` takes a list of *x*-values and a list of *y*-values and plots them. The lists have to have the same length. `xscale` and `yscale` make the axes either linear or logarithmic.

`title`, `xlabel`, and `ylabel` are self-explanatory. Finally, `show` displays the plot on the screen. You could also use `savefig` to save the plot in a file.

Documentation of `pyplot` is available at *http://matplotlib.sourceforge.net/*.

Exercise 3-6.

Test the performance of `LinearMap`, `BetterMap`, and `HashMap`; see if you can characterize their order of growth.

You can download my map implementations from *http://thinkcomplex.com/Map.py* and the code I used in this section from *http://thinkcomplex.com/listsum.py*.

You will have to find a range of n that is big enough to show asymptotic behavior, but small enough to run quickly.

List Comprehensions

One of the most common programming patterns is to traverse a list while building a new list.

Here is an example that computes the square of each element in a list and accumulates the results:

```
res = []
    for x in t:
        res.append(x**2)
```

This pattern is so common that Python provides a more concise syntax for it, called a **list comprehension**. In this context, the sense of "comprehend" is something like "contain" rather than "understand." See *http://en.wikipedia.org/wiki/List_comprehension*. Here's what it looks like:

```
res = [x**2 for x in t]
```

This expression yields the same result as the previous loop. List comprehensions tend to be fast because the loop is executed in C rather than Python. The drawback is that they are harder to debug.

List comprehensions can include an `if` clause that selects a subset of the items. The following example makes a list of the positive elements in t:

```
res = [x for x in t if x > 0]
```

The following is a common idiom for making a list of tuples, where each tuple is a value and a key from a dictionary:

```
res = [(v, k) for k, v in d.iteritems()]
```

In this case, it is safe to use `iteritems` rather than `items` because the loop does not modify the dictionary. Also, it is likely to be faster because it doesn't have to make a list, just an iterator.

It is also possible to nest `for` loops inside a list comprehension. The following example builds a list of `Edges` between each pair of vertices in `vs`:

```
edges = [Edge(v, w) for v in vs for w in vs if v is not w]
```

That's pretty concise, but complicated comprehensions can be hard to read, so use them sparingly.

Exercise 3-7.

Review the methods you wrote in `Graph.py`, and see if any can be rewritten using list comprehensions.

CHAPTER 4

Small World Graphs

Analysis of Graph Algorithms

The order of growth for a graph algorithm is usually expressed as a function of $|V|$, the number of vertices, and $|E|$, the number of edges.

The order of growth for BFS is $O(|V|+|E|)$, which is a convenient way to say that the runtime grows in proportion to either $|V|$ or $|E|$, whichever is "bigger."

To see why, think about these four operations:

Adding a vertex to the queue
> This happens once for each vertex, so the total cost is in $O(|V|)$.

Removing a vertex from the queue
> This happens once for each vertex, so the total cost is in $O(|V|)$.

Marking a vertex "visited"
> This happens once for each vertex, so the total cost is in $O(|V|)$.

Checking whether a vertex is marked
> This happens once each edge, so the total cost is in $O(|E|)$.

Adding them up, we get $O(|V|+|E|)$. If we know the relationship between $|V|$ and $|E|$, we can simplify this expression. For example, in a regular graph, the number of edges is in $O(|V|)$, so BFS is linear in $|V|$. In a complete graph, the number of edges is in $O(|V|^2)$, so BFS is quadratic in $|V|$.

Of course, this analysis is based on the assumption that all four operations—adding and removing vertices, marking and checking marks—are constant time.

Marking vertices is easy. You can add an attribute to the Vertex objects or put the marked ones in a set and use the in operator.

But making a first-in-first-out (FIFO) queue that can add and remove vertices in constant time is not as easy as it sounds.

FIFO Implementation

A FIFO is a data structure that provides the following operations:

append
> Add a new item to the end of the queue.

pop
> Remove and return the item at the front of the queue.

There are several good implementations of this data structure. One is the **doubly-linked list**, which you can read about at *http://en.wikipedia.org/wiki/Doubly-linked_list*. Another is a **circular buffer**, which you can read about at *http://en.wikipedia.org/wiki/Circular_buffer*.

Exercise 4-1.

Write an implementation of a FIFO using either a doubly-linked list or a circular buffer.

Yet another possibility is to use a Python dictionary and two indices: `nextin` keeps track of the back of the queue, and `nextout` keeps track of the front. The dictionary maps from integer indices to values.

Here is an implementation based on Raymond Hettinger's recipe at *http://code.active state.com/recipes/68436/*:

```python
class DictFifo(object):

    def __init__(self):
        self.nextin = 0
        self.nextout = 0
        self.data = {}

    def append(self, value):
        self.data[self.nextin] = value
        self.nextin += 1

    def pop(self, n=-1):
        value = self.data.pop(self.nextout)
        self.nextout += 1
        return value
```

`append` stores the new item and increments `nextin`; both operations are constant time.

`pop` removes the last item and increments `nextout`. Again, both operations are constant time.

As yet another alternative, the Python `collections` module provides an object called a deque, which stands for "double-ended queue." It is supposed to be pronounced "deck," but many people say "deek." A Python deque can be adapted to implement a FIFO.

You can read about deques at *http://en.wikipedia.org/wiki/Deque* and get the details of the Python implementation at *http://docs.python.org/lib/deque-objects.html*.

Exercise 4-2.

The following implementation of a BFS contains two performance errors. What are they? What is the actual order of growth for this algorithm?

```
def bfs(top_node, visit):
    """Breadth-first search on a graph, starting at top_node."""
    visited = set()
    queue = [top_node]
    while len(queue):
        curr_node = queue.pop(0)    # Dequeue
        visit(curr_node)            # Visit the node
        visited.add(curr_node)

        # Enqueue non-visited and non-enqueued children
        queue.extend(c for c in curr_node.children
                     if c not in visited and c not in queue)
```

Test this code with a range of graph sizes and check your analysis. Then use a FIFO implementation to fix the errors and confirm that your algorithm is linear.

Stanley Milgram

Stanley Milgram was an American social psychologist who conducted two of the most famous experiments in social science: the Milgram experiment, which studied people's obedience to authority (*http://en.wikipedia.org/wiki/Milgram_experiment*), and the small world experiment, which studied the structure of social networks (*http://en.wiki pedia.org/wiki/Small_world_phenomenon*).

In the small world experiment, Milgram sent a package to several randomly chosen people in Wichita, Kansas with instructions asking them to forward an enclosed letter to a target person, identified by name and occupation, in Sharon, Massachusetts (which is the town near Boston where I grew up). The subjects were told that they could mail the letter directly to the target person only if they knew him personally; otherwise, they were instructed to send it, and the same instructions, to a relative or friend who they thought would be more likely to know the target person.

Many of the letters were never delivered, but for the ones that were, the average path length—the number of times the letters were forwarded—was about six. This result was taken to confirm previous observations (and speculations) that the typical distance between any two people in a social network is about "six degrees of separation."

This conclusion is surprising because most people expect social networks to be localized—people tend to live near their friends—and in a graph with local connections, path lengths tend to increase in proportion to geographical distance. For example, most of my friends live nearby, so I would guess that the average distance between nodes in a social network is about 50 miles. Wichita is about 1600 miles from Boston, so if Milgram's letters traversed typical links in the social network, they should have taken 32 hops, not 6.

Watts and Strogatz

In 1998, Duncan Watts and Steven Strogatz published a paper in *Nature*, "Collective dynamics of 'small-world' networks," that proposed an explanation for the small world phenomenon. You can download it from *http://www.nature.com/nature/journal/v393/n6684/abs/393440a0.html*.

Watts and Strogatz started with two kinds of graph that were well understood: random graphs and regular graphs. They looked at two properties of these graphs: clustering and path length.

Clustering
> This is a measure of the "cliquishness" of the graph. In a graph, a **clique** is a subset of nodes that are all connected to each other; in a social network, a clique is a set of friends who all know each other. Watts and Strogatz defined a clustering coefficient that quantifies the likelihood that two nodes that are connected to the same node are also connected to each other.

Path length
> This is a measure of the average distance between two nodes, which corresponds to the degrees of separation in a social network.

Their initial result was what you might expect: regular graphs have high clustering and high path lengths, and random graphs with the same size tend to have low clustering and low path lengths. So neither of these is a good model of social networks, which seem to combine high clustering with short path lengths.

Their goal was to create a **generative model** of a social network. A generative model tries to explain a phenomenon by modeling the process that builds or leads to the phenomenon. In this case, Watts and Strogatz proposed a process for building small-world graphs:

1. Start with a regular graph with *n* nodes and degree *k*. Watts and Strogatz start with a ring lattice, which is a kind of regular graph. You could replicate their experiment or try instead a graph that is regular but not a ring lattice.

2. Choose a subset of the edges in the graph and "rewire" them by replacing them with random edges. Again, you could replicate the procedure described in the paper or experiment with alternatives.

The proportion of edges that are rewired is a parameter, p, that controls how random the graph is. With $p = 0$, the graph is regular; with $p = 1$, it is random.

Watts and Strogatz found that small values of p yield graphs with high clustering, like a regular graph, and low path lengths, like a random graph.

Exercise 4-3.

Read the Watts and Strogatz paper, and answer the following questions:

1. What process do Watts and Strogatz use to rewire their graphs?
2. What is the definition of the clustering coefficient $C(p)$?
3. What is the definition of the average path length $L(p)$?
4. What real-world graphs did Watts and Strogatz look at? What evidence do they present that these graphs have the same structure as the graphs generated by their model?

Exercise 4-4.

Create a file named `SmallWorldGraph.py`, and define a class named `SmallWorldGraph` that inherits from `RandomGraph`.

If you did Exercise 2-4, you can use your own `RandomGraph.py`; otherwise, you can download mine from *http://thinkcomplex.com/RandomGraph.py*.

1. Write a method called `rewire` that takes a probability, p, as a parameter, and starting with a regular graph, rewires the graph using Watts and Strogatz's algorithm.
2. Write a method called `clustering_coefficient` that computes and returns the clustering coefficient as defined in the paper.
3. Make a graph that replicates the line marked $C(p)/C(0)$ in Figure 2 of the Watts and Strogatz paper. In other words, confirm that the clustering coefficient drops off slowly for small values of p.

Before we can replicate the other line, we have to learn about shortest path algorithms.

Dijkstra

Edsger W. Dijkstra was a Dutch computer scientist who invented an efficient shortest path algorithm (see *http://en.wikipedia.org/wiki/Dijkstra%27s_algorithm*). He also invented the semaphore, which is a data structure used to coordinate programs that communicate with each other (see *http://en.wikipedia.org/wiki/Semaphore_(programming)* and my book, *The Little Book of Semaphores*).

Dijkstra is famous (and notorious) as the author of a series of essays on computer science. Some, like "A Case Against the GO TO Statement," have had a profound effect on programming practice. Others, like "On the Cruelty of Really Teaching Computing Science," are entertaining in their cantankerousness, but less effective.

Dijkstra's algorithm solves the "single-source shortest path problem," which means that it finds the minimum distance from a given source node to every other node in the graph (or at least every connected node).

We start with a simplified version of the algorithm that considers all edges the same length. The more general version works with any non-negative edge lengths.

The simplified version is similar to the breadth-first search in "Connected Graphs" on page 17, except that instead of marking visited nodes, we label them with their distance from the source. Initially, all nodes are labeled with an infinite distance. Like a breadth-first search, Dijkstra's algorithm uses a queue of discovered unvisited nodes:

1. Give the source node distance 0, and add it to the queue. Give the other nodes infinite distance.
2. Remove a vertex from the queue, and assign its distance to d. Find the vertices it is connected to. For each connected vertex with infinite distance, replace the distance with $d + 1$ and add it to the queue.
3. If the queue is not empty, go back to step 2.

The first time you execute step 2, the only node in the queue has distance 0. The second time, the queue contains all nodes with distance 1. Once those nodes are processed, the queue contains all nodes with distance 2, and so on.

So when a node is discovered for the first time, it is labeled with the distance $d + 1$, which is the shortest path to that node. It is not possible that you will discover a shorter path later, because if there were a shorter path, you would have discovered it sooner. That is not a proof of the correctness of the algorithm, but it sketches the structure of the proof by contradiction.

In the more general case where the edges have different lengths, it is possible to discover a shorter path after you have discovered a longer path, so a little more work is needed.

Exercise 4-5.

Write an implementation of Dijkstra's algorithm and use it to compute the average path length of a SmallWorldGraph.

Make a graph that replicates the line marked $L(p) / L(0)$ in Figure 2 of the Watts and Strogatz paper. Confirm that the average path length drops off quickly for small values of p. What is the range of values for p that yield graphs with high clustering and low path lengths?

Exercise 4-6.

A natural question about the Watts and Strogatz paper is whether the small world phenomenon is specific to their generative model or whether other similar models yield the same qualitative result (high clustering and low path lengths).

To answer this question, choose a variation of the Watts and Strogatz model and replicate their Figure 2. There are two kinds of variation you might consider:

- Instead of starting with a regular graph, start with another graph with high clustering. One option is a locally connected graph where vertices are placed at random locations in the plane and each vertex is connected to its nearest k neighbors.
- Experiment with different kinds of rewiring.

If a range of similar models yield similar behavior, we say that the results of the paper are **robust**.

Exercise 4-7.

To compute the average path length in a SmallWorldGraph, you probably ran Dijkstra's single-source shortest path algorithm for each node in the graph. In effect, you solved the "all-pairs shortest path" problem, which finds the shortest path between all pairs of nodes.

1. Find an algorithm for the all-pairs shortest path problem and implement it. Compare the runtime with your "all-source Dijkstra" algorithm.
2. Which algorithm gives better order-of-growth runtime as a function of the number of vertices and edges? Why do you think Dijkstra's algorithm does better than the order-of-growth analysis suggests?

What Kind of Explanation Is That?

If you ask me why planetary orbits are elliptical, I might start by modeling a planet and a star as point masses. I would look up the law of universal gravitation at *http://en.wikipedia.org/wiki/Newton's_law_of_universal_gravitation* and use it to write a differential equation for the motion of the planet. Then I would either derive the orbit equation or, more likely, look it up at *http://en.wikipedia.org/wiki/Orbit_equation*. With a little algebra, I could derive the conditions that yield an elliptical orbit. Then I would argue that the objects we consider planets satisfy these conditions.

People, or at least scientists, are generally satisfied with this kind of explanation. One of the reasons for its appeal is that the assumptions and approximations in the model seem reasonable. Planets and stars are not really point masses, but the distances between them are so big that their actual sizes are negligible. Planets in the same solar system can affect each others' orbits, but the effect is usually small, and we ignore relativistic effects, again on the assumption that they are small.

This explanation is also appealing because it is equation-based. We can express the orbit equation in a closed form, which means that we can compute orbits efficiently. It also means that we can derive general expressions for the orbital velocity, orbital period, and other quantities.

Finally, I think this kind of explanation is appealing because it has the form of a mathematical proof. It starts from a set of axioms and derives the result by logic and analysis. But it is important to remember that the proof pertains to the model and not the real world. That is, we can prove that an idealized model of a planet yields an elliptical orbit, but we can't prove that the model pertains to actual planets (in fact, it does not).

By comparison, Watts and Strogatz's explanation of the small world phenomenon may seem less satisfying. First, the model is more abstract, which is to say less realistic. Second, the results are generated by simulation, not by mathematical analysis. Finally, the results seem less like a proof and more like an example.

Many of the models in this book are like the Watts and Strogatz model: abstract, simulation-based, and (at least superficially) less formal than conventional mathematical models. One of the goals of this book is to consider the questions these models raise:

- What kind of work can these models do: are they predictive, explanatory, or both?
- Are the explanations these models offer less satisfying than explanations based on more traditional models? Why?
- How should we characterize the differences between these and more conventional models? Are they different in kind or only in degree?

Over the course of the book, I will offer my answers to these questions, but they are tentative and sometimes speculative. I encourage you to consider them skeptically and reach your own conclusions.

CHAPTER 5

Scale-Free Networks

Zipf's Law

Zipf's law describes a relationship between the frequencies and ranks of words in natural languages; see *http://en.wikipedia.org/wiki/Zipf%27s_law*. The "frequency" of a word is the number of times it appears in a body of work. The "rank" of a word is its position in a list of words sorted by frequency. The most common word has rank 1, the second most common has rank 2, etc.

Specifically, Zipf's Law predicts that the frequency, f, of the word with rank r is:

$$f = cr^{-s}$$

where s and c are parameters that depend on the language and the text.

If you take the logarithm of both sides of this equation, you get:

$$\log f = \log c - s \log r$$

So if you plot $\log f$ versus $\log r$, you should get a straight line with slope $-s$ and intercept $\log c$.

Exercise 5-1.

Write a program that reads a text from a file, counts word frequencies, and prints one line for each word in descending order of frequency. You can test it by downloading an out-of-copyright book in plain text format from `http://gutenberg.org`. You might want to remove punctuation first.

If you need some help getting started, you can download *http://thinkcomplex.com/Pmf .py*, which provides an object named `Hist` that maps from value to frequencies.

Plot the results and check whether they form a straight line. For plotting suggestions, see "pyplot" on page 33. Can you estimate the value of s?

You can download my solution from *http://thinkcomplex.com/Zipf.py*.

Cumulative Distributions

A distribution is a statistical description of a set of values. For example, if you collect the population of every city and town in the U.S., you would have a set of about 14,000 integers.

The simplest description of this set is a list of numbers, which would be complete but not very informative. A more concise description is a statistical summary like the mean and variation, but that is not a complete description because there are many sets of values with the same summary statistics.

One alternative is a histogram, which divides the range of possible values into "bins" and counts the number of values that fall in each bin. Histograms are common, so they are easy to understand, but it is tricky to get the bin size right. If the bins are too small, the number of values in each bin is also small, so the histogram doesn't give much insight. If the bins are too large, they lump together a wide range of values, which obscures details that might be important.

A better alternative is a **cumulative distribution function** (CDF), which maps from a value, x, to the fraction of values less than or equal to x. If you choose a value at random, $CDF(x)$ is the probability that the value you get is less than or equal to x.

For a list of n values, the simplest way to compute CDF is to sort the values. Then the CDF of the ith value (starting from 1) is i/n.

I have written a class called Cdf that provides functions for creating and manipulating CDFs. You can download it from *http://thinkcomplex.com/Cdf.py*.

As an example, we'll compute the CDF for the values {1,2,2,4,5}:

```
import Cdf
cdf = Cdf.MakeCdfFromList([1,2,2,4,5])
```

MakeCdfFromList can take any sequence or iterator. Once you have the Cdf, you can find the probability, $CDF(x)$, for a given value:

```
prob = cdf.Prob(2)
```

The result is 0.6, because 3/5 of the values are less than or equal to 2. You can also compute the value for a given probability:

```
value = cdf.Value(0.5)
```

The value with probability 0.5 is the median, which in this example is 2.

To plot the Cdf, you can use Render, which returns a list of value-probability pairs.

```
xs, ps = cdf.Render()
    for x, p in zip(xs, ps):
        print x, p
```

The result is:

```
1 0.0
1 0.2
2 0.2
2 0.6
4 0.6
4 0.8
5 0.8
5 1.0
```

Each value appears twice. That way when we plot the CDF, we get a stair-step pattern.

```
import matplotlib.pyplot as pyplot

xs, ps = cdf.Render()

pyplot.plot(xs, ps, linewidth=3)
pyplot.axis([0.9, 5.1, 0, 1])
pyplot.title('CDF')
pyplot.xlabel('value, x')
pyplot.ylabel('probability, CDF(x)')
pyplot.show()
```

Figure 5-1 shows the CDF for the values {1,2,2,4,5}.

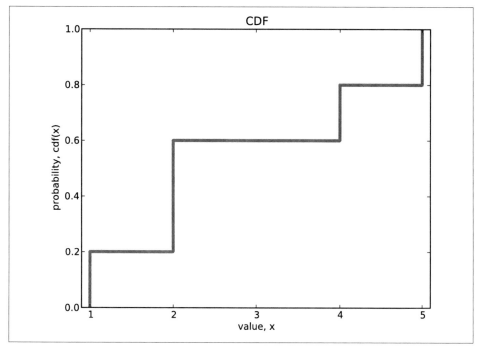

Figure 5-1. CDF of the values {1,2,2,4,5}

I drew vertical lines at each of the values, which is not mathematically correct. To be more rigorous, I should draw a discontinuous function.

Exercise 5-2.

Read the code in `Cdf.py`. What is the order of growth for `MakeCdfFromList` and the methods `Prob` and `Value`?

Continuous Distributions

The distributions we have seen so far are sometimes called **empirical distributions** because they are based on a dataset that comes from some kind of empirical observation.

An alternative is a **continuous distribution**, which is characterized by a CDF that is a continuous function. Some of these distributions, like the Gaussian or normal distribution, are well known, at least to people who have studied statistics. Many real-world phenomena can be approximated by continuous distributions, which is why they are useful.

For example, if you observe a mass of radioactive material with an instrument that can detect decay events, the distribution of times between events will most likely fit an exponential distribution. The same is true for any series where an event is equally likely at any time.

The CDF of the exponential distribution is:

$$CDF(x) = 1 - e^{-\lambda x}$$

The parameter, λ, determines the mean and variance of the distribution. This equation can be used to derive a simple visual test for whether a dataset can be well approximated by an exponential distribution. All you have to do is plot the **complementary distribution** on a log-y scale.

The complementary distribution (CCDF) is just $1 - CDF(x)$; if you plot the complementary distribution of a dataset that you think is exponential, you expect to see a function like this:

$$y = 1 - CDF(x) \sim e^{-\lambda x}$$

If you take the log of both sides of this equation, you get:

$$\log y \sim -\lambda x$$

So on a log-y scale, the CCDF should look like a straight line with slope $-\lambda$.

Exercise 5-3.

Write a function called `plot_ccdf` that takes a list of values and the corresponding list of probabilities and plots the CCDF on a log-y scale.

To test your function, use `expovariate` from the `random` module to generate 100 values from an exponential distribution. Plot the CCDF on a log-y scale, and see if it falls on a straight line.

Pareto Distributions

The Pareto distribution is named after the economist Vilfredo Pareto, who used it to describe the distribution of wealth; see *http://en.wikipedia.org/wiki/Pareto_distribu tion*. Since then, people have used it to describe phenomena in the natural and social sciences, including sizes of cities and towns, of sand particles and meteorites, and of forest fires and earthquakes.

The Pareto distribution is characterized by a CDF with the following form:

$$1 - \left(\frac{x}{x_m} \right)^{-\alpha}$$

The parameters x_m and α determine the location and shape of the distribution. x_m is the minimum possible value.

Values from a Pareto distribution often have these properties:

Long tail
    Pareto distributions contain many small values and a few very large ones.

80/20 rule
    The large values in a Pareto distribution are so large that they make up a dispro-portionate share of the total. In the context of wealth, the 80/20 rule says that 20% of the people own 80% of the wealth.

Scale free
    Short-tailed distributions are centered around a typical size, which is called a "scale." For example, the great majority of adult humans are between 100 and 200 cm in height, so we could say that the scale of human height is a few hundred centimeters. But for long-tailed distributions, there is no similar range (bounded by a factor of two) that contains the bulk of the distribution. So we say that these distributions are "scale-free."

To get a sense of the difference between the Pareto and Gaussian distributions, imagine what the world would be like if the distribution of human height were Pareto.

In Pareto World, the shortest person is 100 cm, and the median is 150 cm, so that part of the distribution is not very different from ours. But if you generate 6 billion values from this distribution, the tallest person might be 100 km—that's what it means to be scale-free!

There is a simple visual test that indicates whether an empirical distribution is well-characterized by a Pareto distribution: on a log-log scale, the CCDF looks like a straight line. The derivation is similar to what we saw in the previous section.

The equation for the CCDF is:

$$y = 1 - CDF(x) \sim \left(\frac{x}{x_m}\right)^{-\alpha}$$

Taking the log of both sides yields:

$$\log y \sim -\alpha(\log x - \log x_m)$$

So if you plot $\log y$ versus $\log x$, it should look like a straight line with slope $-\alpha$ and intercept $\alpha \log x_m$.

Exercise 5-4.

Write a version of `plot_ccdf` that plots the complementary CCDF on a log-log scale.

To test your function, use `paretovariate` from the `random` module to generate 100 values from a Pareto distribution. Plot the CCDF on a log-y scale and see if it falls on a straight line. What happens to the curve as you increase the number of values?

Exercise 5-5.

The distribution of populations for cities and towns has been proposed as an example of a real-world phenomenon that can be described with a Pareto distribution.

The U.S. Census Bureau publishes data on the population of every incorporated city and town in the United States. I wrote a small program that downloads this data and converts it into a convenient form. You can download it from *http://thinkcomplex.com/populations.py*.

Read over the program to make sure you know what it does, and then write a program that computes and plots the distribution of populations for the 14,593 cities and towns in the dataset.

Plot the CDF on linear and log-x scales so you can get a sense of the shape of the distribution. Then plot the CCDF on a log-log scale to see if it has the characteristic shape of a Pareto distribution.

What conclusion do you draw about the distribution of sizes for cities and towns?

Barabási and Albert

In 1999, Barabási and Albert published a paper in *Science* called "Emergence of Scaling in Random Networks," which characterizes the structure (also called "topology") of several real-world networks, including graphs that represent the interconnectivity of movie actors, World Wide Web (WWW) pages, and elements in the electrical power grid in the western United States. You can download the paper from *http://www.scien cemag.org/content/286/5439/509*.

They measure the degree (number of connections) of each node and compute $P(k)$, the probability that a vertex has degree k; then they plot $P(k)$ versus k on a log-log scale. The tail of the plot fits a straight line, so they conclude that it obeys a **power law**; that is, as k gets large, $P(k)$ is asymptotic to $k^{-\gamma}$, where γ is a parameter that determines the rate of decay.

They also propose a model that generates random graphs with the same property. The essential features of the model that distinguish it from the Erdős-Rényi model and the Watts-Strogatz model are:

Growth

> Instead of starting with a fixed number of vertices, Barabási and Albert start with a small graph and add vertices gradually.

Preferential attachment

> When a new edge is created, it is more likely to connect to a vertex that already has a large number of edges. This "rich get richer" effect is characteristic of the growth patterns of some real-world networks.

Finally, they show that graphs generated by this model have a distribution of degrees that obeys a power law. Graphs that have this property are sometimes called **scale-free networks**; see *http://en.wikipedia.org/wiki/Scale-free_network*. That name can be confusing because it is the distribution of degrees that is scale-free, not the network.

In order to maximize confusion, distributions that obey the power law are sometimes called **scaling distributions** because they are invariant under a change of scale. That means that if you change the units in which the quantities are expressed, the slope parameter, γ, doesn't change. You can read *http://en.wikipedia.org/wiki/Power_law* for the details, but it is not important for what we are doing here.

Exercise 5-6.

This exercise asks you to make connections between the Watts-Strogatz (WS) and Barabási-Albert (BA) models.

1. Read Barabási and Albert's paper, and implement their algorithm for generating graphs. See if you can replicate their Figure 2(A), which shows $P(k)$ versus k for a graph with 150,000 vertices.

2. Use the WS model to generate the largest graph you can in a reasonable amount of time. Plot $P(k)$ versus k, and see if you can characterize the tail behavior.

3. Use the BA model to generate a graph with about 1,000 vertices, and compute the characteristic length and clustering coefficient as defined in the Watts and Strogatz paper. Do scale-free networks have the characteristics of a small world graph?

Zipf, Pareto, and Power Laws

At this point, we have seen three phenomena that yield a straight line on a log-log plot:

Zipf plot
> Frequency as a function of rank

Pareto CCDF
> The complementary CDF of a Pareto distribution

Power law plot
> A histogram of frequencies

The similarity in these plots is not a coincidence; these visual tests are closely related.

Starting with a power law distribution, we have:

$$P(k) \sim k^{-\gamma}$$

If we choose a random node in a scale free network, $P(k)$ is the probability that its degree equals k.

The cumulative distribution function, $CDF(k)$, is the probability that the degree is less than or equal to k, so we can get that by summation:

$$CDF(k) = \sum_{i=0}^{k} P(i)$$

For large values of k, we can approximate the summation with an integral:

$$\sum_{i=0}^{k} i^{-\gamma} \sim \int_{i=0}^{k} i^{-\gamma} = \frac{1}{\gamma - 1}(1 - k^{-\gamma+1})$$

To make this a proper CDF, we could normalize it so that it goes to 1 as k goes to infinity, but that's not necessary because all we need to know is:

$$CDF(k) \sim 1 - k^{-\gamma+1}$$

This shows that the distribution of k is asymptotic to a Pareto distribution with $\alpha = \gamma - 1$.

Similarly, if we start with a straight line on a Zipf plot,[1] we have:

$$f = cr^{-s}$$

where f is the frequency of the word with rank r. Inverting this relationship yields:

$$r = (f/c)^{-1/s}$$

Now subtracting 1 and dividing through by the number of different words, n, we get:

$$\frac{r-1}{n} = \frac{(f/c)^{-1/s}}{n} - \frac{1}{n}$$

This is only interesting because if r is the rank of a word, then $(r-1)/n$ is the fraction of words with lower ranks, which is the fraction of words with higher frequency, which is the CCDF of the distribution of frequencies:

$$CCDF(x) = \frac{(f/c)^{-1/s}}{n} - \frac{1}{n}$$

To characterize the asymptotic behavior for large n, we can ignore c and $1/n$, which yields:

$$CCDF(x) \sim f^{-1/s}$$

This shows that if a set of words obeys Zipf's law, the distribution of their frequencies is asymptotic to a Pareto distribution with $\alpha = 1/s$.

So the three visual tests are mathematically equivalent; a dataset that passes one test will pass all three. But as a practical matter, the power law plot is noisier than the other two because it is the derivative of the CCDF.

The Zipf and CCDF plots are more robust, but Zipf's law is only applicable to discrete data (like words), not continuous quantities. CCDF plots work with both.

For these reasons—robustness and generality—I recommend using CCDFs.

---

1. This derivation follows Adamic, "Zipf, power law and Pareto—a ranking tutorial," available at *http://www.hpl.hp.com/research/idl/papers/ranking/ranking.html*.

Exercise 5-7.

The Stanford Large Network Dataset Collection is a repository of datasets from a variety of networks, including social networks, communication and collaboration, Internet, and road networks. See *http://snap.stanford.edu/data/index.html*.

Download one of these datasets and explore. Is there evidence of small world behavior? Is the network scale-free? What else can you discover?

Explanatory Models

We started the discussion of networks with Milgram's small world experiment, which shows that path lengths in social networks are surprisingly small; hence the phrase "six degrees of separation."

When we see something surprising, it is natural to ask "why?", but sometimes it's not clear what kind of answer we are looking for. One kind of answer is an **explanatory model** (see Figure 5-2). The logical structure of an explanatory model is:

1. In a system, S, we see something observable, O, that warrants explanation.
2. We construct a model, M, that is analogous to the system; that is, there is a correspondence between the elements of the model and the elements of the system.
3. By simulation or mathematical derivation, we show that the model exhibits a behavior, B, that is analogous to O.
4. We conclude that S exhibits O *because* S is similar to M, M exhibits B, and B is similar to O.

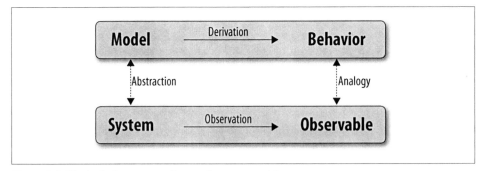

Figure 5-2. The logical structure of an explanatory model

At its core, this is an argument by analogy, which says that if two things are similar in some ways, they are likely to be similar in other ways. Argument by analogy can be useful, and explanatory models can be satisfying, but they do not constitute a proof in the mathematical sense of the word.

Remember that all models leave out (or "abstract away") details that we think are unimportant. For any system, there are many possible models that include or ignore different features. Also, there might be models that exhibit different behaviors—B, B', and B"—that are similar to O in different ways. In that case, which model explains O?

The small world phenomenon is an example: the Watts-Strogatz (WS) model and the Barabási-Albert (BA) model both exhibit small world behavior, but they offer different explanations:

- The WS model suggests that social networks are small because they include both strongly connected clusters and "weak ties" that connect clusters (see *http://en .wikipedia.org/wiki/Mark_Granovetter*).

- The BA model suggests that social networks are small because they include nodes with high degrees that act as hubs, and that hubs grow over time due to preferential attachment.

As is often the case in young areas of science, the problem is not that we have no explanations, but that we have too many.

Exercise 5-8.

Are these explanations compatible; that is, can they both be right? Which do you find more satisfying as an explanation, and why?

Is there data you could collect or experiments you could perform that would provide evidence in favor of one model over the other?

Choosing among competing models is the topic of Thomas Kuhn's essay, "Objectivity, Value Judgment, and Theory Choice." Kuhn was a historian of science who wrote *The Structure of Scientific Revolutions* in 1962, and spent the rest of his life explaining what he meant to say.

What criteria does Kuhn propose for choosing among competing models? Do these criteria influence your opinion about the WS and BA models? Are there other criteria you think should be considered?

CHAPTER 6

Cellular Automata

A cellular automaton is a model of a world with very simple physics. "Cellular" means that the space is divided into discrete chunks, called cells. An "automaton" is a machine that performs computations—it could be a real machine, but more often the "machine" is a mathematical abstraction or a computer simulation.

Automata are governed by rules that determine how the system evolves in time. Time is divided into discrete steps, and the rules specify how to compute the state of the world during the next time step based on the current state.

As a trivial example, consider a cellular automaton (CA) with a single cell. The state of the cell is an integer represented by the variable x_i, where the subscript i indicates that x_i is the state of the system during time step i. As an initial condition, $x_0 = 0$.

Now all we need is a rule. Arbitrarily, I'll pick $x_i = x_{i-1} + 1$, which says that after each time step, the state of the CA gets incremented by 1. So far, we have a simple CA that performs a simple calculation: it counts.

But this CA is atypical; normally the number of possible states is finite. To bring it into line, I'll choose the smallest interesting number of states, two, and another simple rule, $x_i = (x_{i-1} + 1)\%2$, where % is the remainder (or modulus) operator.

This CA performs a simple calculation: it blinks (that is, the state of the cell switches between 0 and 1 after every time step).

Most CAs are **deterministic**, which means that rules do not have any random elements; given the same initial state, they always produce the same result. There are also non-deterministic CAs, but I will not address them here.

Stephen Wolfram

The CA in the previous section was zero-dimensional, and it wasn't very interesting. But one-dimensional CAs turn out to be surprisingly interesting.

In the early 1980s, Stephen Wolfram published a series of papers presenting a systematic study of one-dimensional CAs. He identified four general categories of behavior, each more interesting than the last.

To say that a CA has dimensions is to say that the cells are arranged in a contiguous space so that some of them are considered neighbors. In one dimension, there are three natural configurations:

Finite sequence
> This is a finite number of cells arranged in a row. All cells except the first and last have two neighbors.

Ring
> This is a finite number of cells arranged in a ring. All cells have two neighbors.

Infinite sequence
> This is an infinite number of cells arranged in a row.

The rules that determine how the system evolves in time are based on the notion of a "neighborhood," which is the set of cells that determines the next state of a given cell. Wolfram's experiments use a three-cell neighborhood: the cell itself and its left and right neighbors.

In these experiments, the cells have two states, denoted 0 and 1, so the rules can be summarized by a table that maps from the state of the neighborhood (a tuple of three states) to the next state for the center cell. The following table shows an example:

prev	111	110	101	100	011	010	001	000
next	0	0	1	1	0	0	1	0

The first row shows the eight states a neighborhood can be in. The second row shows the state of the center cell during the next time step. As a concise encoding of this table, Wolfram suggested reading the bottom row as a binary number. Because 00110010 in binary is 50 in decimal, Wolfram calls this CA "Rule 50."

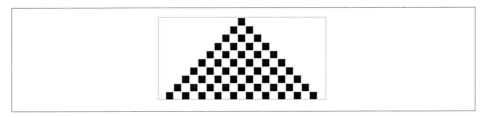

Figure 6-1. Rule 50 after 10 time steps

Figure 6-1 shows the effect of Rule 50 over 10 time steps. The first row shows the state of the system during the first time step; it starts with one cell "on" and the rest "off." The second row shows the state of the system during the next time step, and so on.

The triangular shape in the figure is typical of these CAs; it is a consequence of the shape of the neighborhood. In one time step, each cell influences the state of one neighbor in either direction. During the next time step, that influence can propagate one more cell in each direction. So each cell in the past has a "triangle of influence" that includes all of the cells that can be affected by it.

Implementing CAs

To generate the previous figure, I wrote a Python program that implements and draws CAs. You can download my code from *http://thinkcomplex.com/CA.py* and *http://think complex.com/CADrawer.py*.

To store the state of the CA, I use a NumPy array. An array is a multidimensional data structure whose elements are all of the same type. It is similar to a nested list, but usually smaller and faster. Figure 6-2 shows why. The diagram on the left shows a list of lists of integers; each dot represents a reference, which takes up 4–8 bytes. To access one of the integers, you have to follow two references.

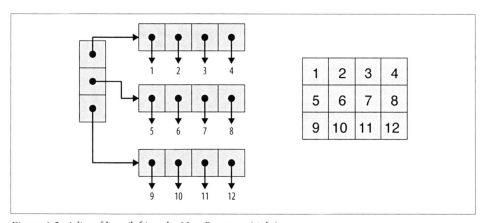

Figure 6-2. A list of lists (left) and a NumPy array (right)

The diagram on the right shows an array of the same integers. Because the elements are all the same size, they can be stored contiguously in memory. This arrangement saves space because it doesn't use references, and it saves time because the location of an element can be computed directly from the indices; there is no need to follow a series of references.

Here is a CA object that uses a NumPy array:

```
import numpy

class CA(object):

    def __init__(self, rule, n=100, ratio=2):
        self.table = make_table(rule)
        self.n = n
        self.m = ratio*n + 1
        self.array = numpy.zeros((n, self.m), dtype=numpy.int8)
        self.next = 0
```

rule is an integer in the range 0-255, which represents the CA rule table using Wolfram's encoding. make_table converts the rule to a dictionary that maps from neighborhood states to cell states. For example, in Rule 50, the table maps from (1,1,1) to 0.

n is the number of rows in the array, which is the number of time steps we will compute. m is the number of columns, which is the number of cells. To get started, I'll implement a finite array of cells.

zeros is provided by NumPy; it creates a new array with the given dimensions, n by m. dtype stands for "data type," and it specifies the type of the array elements. int8 is an 8-bit integer, so we are limited to 256 states, but that's no problem: we only need 2.

next is the index of the next time step.

There are two common starting conditions for CAs: a single cell or a row of random cells. start_single initializes the first row with a single cell and increments next:

```
def start_single(self):
    """Starts with one cell in the middle of the top row."""
    self.array[0, self.m/2] = 1
    self.next += 1
```

The array index is a tuple that specifies the row and column of the cell, in that order.

step computes the next state of the CA:

```
def step(self):
    i = self.next
    self.next += 1

    a = self.array
    t = self.table
    for j in xrange(1,self.m-1):
        a[i,j] = t[tuple(a[i-1, j-1:j+2])]
```

i is the time step and the index of the row we are about to compute. j loops through the cells, skipping the first and last, which are always off.

Arrays support slice operations, so self.array[i-1, j-1:j+2] gets three elements from row i-1. Then we look up the neighborhood tuple in the table, get the next state, and store it in the array.

Array indexing is constant time, so step is linear in n. Filling in the whole array is $O(nm)$.

You can read more about NumPy and arrays at *http://scipy.org/Tentative_NumPy_Tu torial*.

CADrawer

An **abstract class** is a class definition that specifies the interface for a set of methods without providing an implementation. Child classes extend the abstract class and implement the incomplete methods. See *http://en.wikipedia.org/wiki/Abstract_type*.

As an example CADrawer defines an interface for drawing CAs. Here is its definition:

```
class Drawer(object):
    """Drawer is an abstract class that should not be instantiated.
    It defines the interface for a CA drawer; child classes of Drawer
    should implement draw, show and save.

    If draw_array is not overridden, the child class should provide
    draw_cell.
    """
    def __init__(self):
        msg = 'CADrawer is an abstract type and should not be instantiated.'
        raise UnimplementedMethodException, msg

    def draw(self, ca):
        """Draws a representation of cellular automaton (CA).
        This function generally has no visible effect."""
        raise UnimplementedMethodException

    def draw_array(self, a):
        """Iterate through array (a) and draws any non-zero cells."""
        for i in xrange(self.rows):
            for j in xrange(self.cols):
                if a[i,j]:
                    self.draw_cell(j, self.rows-i-1)

    def draw_cell(self, ca):
        """Draws a single cell.
        Not required for all implementations."""
        raise UnimplementedMethodException

    def show(self):
        """Displays the representation on the screen, if possible."""
        raise UnimplementedMethodException

    def save(self, filename):
        """Saves the representation of the CA in filename."""
        raise UnimplementedMethodException
```

Abstract classes should not be instantiated; if you try, you get an Unimplemented MethodException, which is a simple extension of Exception:

```
class UnimplementedMethodException(Exception):
    """Used to indicate that a child class has not implemented an
    abstract method."""
```

To instantiate a CADrawer, you have to define a child class that implements the methods, then instantiate the child.

CADrawer.py provides three implementations: one that uses pyplot, one that uses the Python Imaging Library (PIL), and one that generates Encapsulated Postscript (EPS).

Here is an example that uses PyplotDrawer to display a CA on the screen:

```
ca = CA(rule, n)
    ca.start_single()
    ca.loop(n-1)

    drawer = CADrawer.PyplotDrawer()
    drawer.draw(ca)
    drawer.show()
```

Exercise 6-1.

Download *http://thinkcomplex.com/CA.py* and *http://thinkcomplex.com/CADrawer .py*, and confirm that they run on your system; you might have to install additional Python packages.

Create a new class called CircularCA that extends CA so that the cells are arranged in a ring. Hint: you might find it useful to add a column of "ghost cells" to the array.

You can download my solution from *http://thinkcomplex.com/CircularCA.py*.

Classifying CAs

Wolfram proposes that the behavior of CAs can be grouped into four classes. Class 1 contains the simplest (and least interesting) CAs, the ones that evolve from almost any starting condition to the same uniform pattern. As a trivial example, Rule 0 always generates an empty pattern after one time step.

Rule 50 is an example of Class 2. It generates a simple pattern with a nested structure; that is, the pattern contains many smaller versions of itself. Rule 18 makes the nested structure even clearer; Figure 6-3 shows what it looks like after 64 steps.

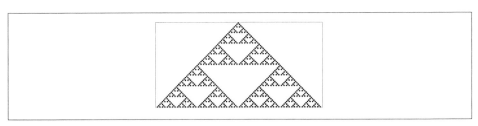

Figure 6-3. Rule 18 after 64 steps

This pattern resembles the Sierpiński triangle, which you can read about at *http://en .wikipedia.org/wiki/Sierpinski_triangle*.

Some Class 2 CAs generate patterns that are intricate and pretty, but compared to Classes 3 and 4, they are relatively simple.

Randomness

Class 3 contains CAs that generate randomness. Rule 30 is an example; Figure 6-4 shows what it looks like after 100 time steps.

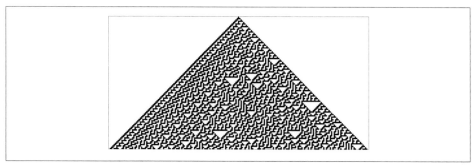

Figure 6-4. Rule 30 after 100 time steps

Along the left side there is an apparent pattern, and on the right side there are triangles in various sizes, but the center seems quite random. In fact, if you take the center column and treat it as a sequence of bits, it is hard to distinguish from a truly random sequence. It passes many of the statistical tests people use to test whether a sequence of bits is random.

Programs that produce random-seeming numbers are called **pseudo-random number generators** (PRNGs). They are not considered truly random for the following reasons:

- Many of them produce sequences with regularities that can be detected statistically. For example, the original implementation of `rand` in the C library used a linear congruential generator that yielded sequences with easily detectable serial correlations.

- Any PRNG that uses a finite amount of state (that is, storage) will eventually repeat itself. One of the characteristics of a generator is the **period** of this repetition.

- The underlying process is fundamentally deterministic, unlike some physical processes (like radioactive decay and thermal noise) that are considered to be fundamentally random.

Modern PRNGs produce sequences that are statistically indistinguishable from random, and they can be implemented with periods so long that the universe will collapse before they repeat. The existence of these generators raises the question of whether there is any real difference between a good quality pseudo-random sequence and a sequence generated by a "truly" random process. In *A New Kind of Science*, Wolfram argues that there is not (pages 315–326).

Exercise 6-2.

This exercise asks you to implement and test several PRNGs.

1. Write a program that implements one of the linear congruential generators described at *http://en.wikipedia.org/wiki/Linear_congruential_generator*.

2. Download DieHarder, a random number test suite, from *http://phy.duke.edu/~rgb/ General/rand_rate.php* and use it to test your PRNG. How does it do?

3. Read the documentation of Python's random module. What PRNG does it use? Test it using DieHarder.

4. Implement a Rule 30 CA on a ring with a few hundred cells, run it for as many time steps as you can in a reasonable amount of time, and output the center column as a sequence of bits. Test it using DieHarder.

Determinism

The existence of Class 3 CAs is surprising. To understand how surprising, it is useful to consider philosophical **determinism** (see *http://en.wikipedia.org/wiki/Determin ism*). Most philosophical stances are hard to define precisely because they come in a variety of flavors. I often find it useful to define them with a list of statements ordered from weak to strong:

D1
> Deterministic models can make accurate predictions for some physical systems.

D2
> Many physical systems can be modeled by deterministic processes, but some are intrinsically random.

D3
> All events are caused by prior events, but many physical systems are nevertheless fundamentally unpredictable.

D4
> All events are caused by prior events, and can (at least in principle) be predicted.

My goal in constructing this range is to make D1 so weak that virtually everyone would accept it, and D4 so strong that almost no one would accept it, with intermediate statements that some people accept.

The center of mass of world opinion swings along this range in response to historical developments and scientific discoveries. Prior to the scientific revolution, many people regarded the working of the universe as fundamentally unpredictable or controlled by supernatural forces. After the triumphs of Newtonian mechanics, some optimists came to believe something like D4. For example, in 1814, Pierre-Simon Laplace wrote:

> We may regard the present state of the universe as the effect of its past and the cause of its future. An intellect which at a certain moment would know all forces that set nature in motion, and all positions of all items of which nature is composed, if this intellect were also vast enough to submit these data to analysis, it would embrace in a single formula the movements of the greatest bodies of the universe and those of the tiniest atom; for such an intellect nothing would be uncertain and the future just like the past would be present before its eyes.

This intellect came to be called "Laplace's demon" (see *http://en.wikipedia.org/wiki/Laplace's_demon*). The word "demon" in this context has the sense of "spirit," with no implication of evil.

Discoveries in the 19th and 20th centuries gradually dismantled this hope. The thermodynamic concept of entropy, radioactive decay, and quantum mechanics posed successive challenges to strong forms of determinism.

In the 1960s, chaos theory showed that in some deterministic systems, prediction is only possible over short time scales, limited by the precision of measurement of initial conditions.

Most of these systems are continuous in space (if not time) and nonlinear, so the complexity of their behavior is not entirely surprising. Wolfram's demonstration of complex behavior in simple cellular automata is more surprising—and disturbing, at least to a deterministic world view.

So far I have focused on scientific challenges to determinism, but the longest-standing objection is the conflict between determinism and human free will. Complexity science provides a possible resolution of this apparent conflict; we come back to this topic in "Free Will" on page 104.

Structures

The behavior of Class 4 CAs is even more surprising. Several 1-D CAs, most notably Rule 110, are **Turing complete**, which means that they can compute any computable function. This property, also called **universality**, was proved by Matthew Cook in 1998. See *http://en.wikipedia.org/wiki/Rule_110*.

Figure 6-5 shows what Rule 110 looks like with an initial condition of a single cell and 100 time steps. At this time scale, it is not apparent that anything special is going on. There are some regular patterns but also some features that are hard to characterize.

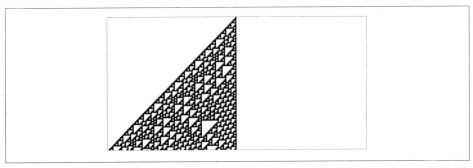

Figure 6-5. Rule 110 after 100 time steps

Figure 6-6 shows a bigger picture, starting with a random initial condition and 600 time steps.

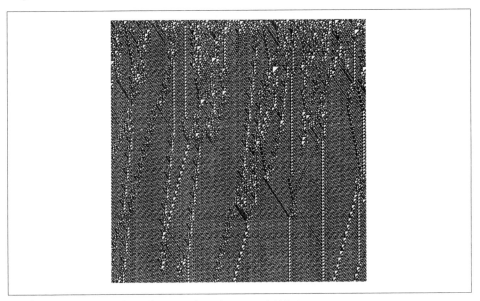

Figure 6-6. Rule 110 with random initial conditions and 600 time steps

After about 100 steps, the background settles into a simple repeating pattern, but there are a number of persistent structures that appear as disturbances in the background. Some of these structures are stable, so they appear as vertical lines. Others translate in space, appearing as diagonals with different slopes depending on how many time steps they take to shift by one column. These structures are called **spaceships**.

Collisions between spaceships yield different results depending on the types of the spaceships and the phase they are in when they collide. Some collisions annihilate both ships, others leave one ship unchanged, and still others yield one or more ships of different types.

These collisions are the basis of computation in a Rule 110 CA. If you think of space-ships as signals that propagate on wires, and collisions as gates that compute logical operations like AND and OR, you can see what it means for a CA to perform a computation.

Exercise 6-3.

This exercise asks you to experiment with Rule 110 and see how many spaceships you can find.

1. Modify your program from the previous exercises so it starts with an initial condition that yields the stable background pattern.

2. Modify the initial condition by adding different patterns in the center of the row, and see which ones yield spaceships. You might want to enumerate all possible patterns of n bits for some reasonable value of n. For each spaceship, can you find the period and rate of translation? What is the biggest spaceship you can find?

Universality

To understand universality, we have to understand computability theory, which is about models of computation and what they compute.

One of the most general models of computation is the Turing machine, which is an abstract computer proposed by Alan Turing in 1936. A Turing machine is a 1-D CA, infinite in both directions, augmented with a read-write head. At any time, the head is positioned over a single cell. It can read the state of that cell (usually there are only two states), and it can write a new value into the cell.

In addition, the machine has a register, which records the state of the machine (one of a finite number of states), and a table of rules. For each machine state and cell state, the table specifies an action. Actions include modifying the cell the head is over, and moving one cell to the left or right.

A Turing machine is not a practical design for a computer, but it models common computer architectures. For a given program running on a real computer, it is possible (at least in principle) to construct a Turing machine that performs an equivalent computation.

The Turing machine is useful because it is possible to characterize the set of functions that can be computed by a Turing machine, which is what Turing did. Functions in this set are called Turing computable.

To say that a Turing machine can compute any Turing-computable function is a **tautology**: it is true by definition. But Turing computability is more interesting than that. It turns out that just about every reasonable model of computation anyone has come up with is Turing complete; that is, it can compute exactly the same set of functions as the Turing machine. Some of these models, like lambda calculus, are very different from a Turing machine, so their equivalence is surprising.

This observation led to the Church-Turing thesis, which is essentially a definition of what it means to be computable. The thesis is that Turing computability is the right (or at least natural) definition of computability, because it describes the power of such a diverse collection of models of computation.

The Rule 110 CA is yet another model of computation, remarkable for its simplicity. That it, too, turns out to be universal lends support to the Church-Turing thesis.

In *A New Kind of Science*, Wolfram states a variation of this thesis, which he calls the "principle of computational equivalence":

> Almost all processes that are not obviously simple can be viewed as computations of equivalent sophistication.

> More specifically, the principle of computational equivalence says that systems found in the natural world can perform computations up to a maximal ("universal") level of computational power, and that most systems do in fact attain this maximal level of computational power. Consequently, most systems are computationally equivalent.[1]

Applying these definitions to CAs, Classes 1 and 2 are obviously simple. It may be less obvious that Class 3 is simple, but in a way, perfect randomness is as simple as perfect order; complexity happens in between. So Wolfram's claim is that Class 4 behavior is common in the natural world and almost all of the systems that manifest it are computationally equivalent.

Exercise 6-4.

The goal of this exercise is to implement a Turing machine. See *http://en.wikipedia.org/wiki/Turing_machine*.

1. Start with a copy of `CA.py` named `TM.py`. Add attributes to represent the location of the head, the action table, and the state register.
2. Override `step` to implement a Turing machine update.
3. For the action table, use the rules for a three-state busy beaver.
4. Write a class named `TMDrawer` that generates an image that represents the state of the tape and the position and state of the head. For one example of what that might look like, see *http://mathworld.wolfram.com/TuringMachine.html*.

---

1. See *http://mathworld.wolfram.com/PrincipleofComputationalEquivalence.html*.

Falsifiability

Wolfram holds that his principle is a stronger claim than the Church-Turing thesis because it is about the natural world rather than abstract models of computation. But saying that natural processes "can be viewed as computations" strikes me more as a statement about theory choice than a hypothesis about the natural world.

Also, with qualifications like "almost" and undefined terms like "obviously simple," his hypothesis may be **unfalsifiable**. Falsifiability is an idea from the philosophy of science, proposed by Karl Popper as a demarcation between scientific hypotheses and pseudoscience. A hypothesis is falsifiable if there is an experiment, at least in the realm of practicality, that would contradict the hypothesis if it were false.

For example, the claim that all life on earth is descended from a common ancestor is falsifiable because it makes specific predictions about similarities in the genetics of modern species (among other things). If we discovered a new species whose DNA was almost entirely different from ours, that would contradict (or at least bring into question) the theory of universal common descent.

On the other hand, special creation—the claim that all species were created in their current form by a supernatural agent—is unfalsifiable because there is nothing that we could observe about the natural world that would contradict it. Any outcome of any experiment could be attributed to the will of the creator.

Unfalsifiable hypotheses can be appealing because they are impossible to refute. If your goal is never to be proved wrong, you should choose hypotheses that are as unfalsifiable as possible.

But if your goal is to make reliable predictions about the world—and this is at least one of the goals of science—then unfalsifiable hypotheses are useless. The problem is that they have no consequences (if they had consequences, they would be falsifiable).

For example, if the theory of special creation were true, what good would it do me to know it? It wouldn't tell me anything about the creator except that he has an "inordinate fondness for beetles" (attributed to J. B. S. Haldane). Unlike the theory of common descent, which informs many areas of science and bioengineering, it would be of no use for understanding the world or acting in it.

Exercise 6-5.

Falsifiability is an appealing and useful idea, but among philosophers of science it is not generally accepted as a solution to the demarcation problem, as Popper claimed.

Read *http://en.wikipedia.org/wiki/Falsifiability*, and answer the following questions:

1. What is the demarcation problem?
2. How, according to Popper, does falsifiability solve the demarcation problem?
3. Give an example of two theories, one considered scientific and one considered unscientific, that are successfully distinguished by the criterion of falsifiability.

4. Can you summarize one or more of the objections that philosophers and historians of science have raised to Popper's claim?

5. Do you get the sense that practicing philosophers think highly of Popper's work?

What Is This a Model Of?

Some cellular automata are primarily mathematical artifacts. They are interesting because they are surprising, useful, or pretty, or because they provide tools for creating new mathematics (like the Church-Turing thesis).

But it is not clear that they are models of physical systems. If they are, they are highly abstracted, which is to say that they are not very detailed or realistic.

For example, some species of cone snail produce a pattern on their shells that resembles the patterns generated by cellular automata (see *http://en.wikipedia.org/wiki/Cone_snail*). It is natural to suppose that a CA is a model of the mechanism that produces patterns on shells as they grow. But, at least initially, it is not clear how the elements of the model (so-called cells, communication between neighbors, rules) correspond to the elements of a growing snail (real cells, chemical signals, protein interaction networks).

For conventional physical models, being realistic is a virtue, at least up to a point. If the elements of a model correspond to the elements of a physical system, there is an obvious analogy between the model and the system. In general, we expect a model that is more realistic to make better predictions and to provide more believable explanations.

Of course, this is only true up to a point. Models that are more detailed are harder to work with and often less amenable to analysis. At some point, a model becomes so complex that it is easier to experiment with the system.

At the other extreme, simple models can be compelling exactly because they are simple.

Simple models offer a different kind of explanation than detailed models. With a detailed model, the argument goes something like this: "We are interested in physical system S, so we construct a detailed model, M, and show by analysis and simulation that M exhibits a behavior, B, that is similar (qualitatively or quantitatively) to an observation of the real system, O. So why does O happen? Because S is similar to M, and B is similar to O, and we can prove that M leads to B."

With simple models we can't claim that S is similar to M, because it isn't. Instead, the argument goes like this: "There is a set of models that share a common set of features. Any model that has these features exhibits behavior B. If we make an observation, O, that resembles B, one way to explain it is to show that the system, S, has the set of features sufficient to produce B."

For this kind of argument, adding more features doesn't help. Making the model more realistic doesn't make the model more reliable; it only obscures the difference between the essential features that cause O and the incidental features that are particular to S.

Figure 6-7 shows the logical structure of this kind of model. The features *x* and *y* are sufficient to produce the behavior. Adding more detail, like features *w* and *z*, might make the model more realistic, but that realism adds no explanatory power.

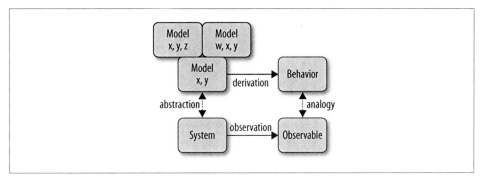

Figure 6-7. The logical structure of a simple physical model

CHAPTER 7

Game of Life

One of the first cellular automata to be studied (and probably the most popular of all time) is a 2D CA called "The Game of Life," or GoL for short. It was developed by John H. Conway and popularized in 1970 in Martin Gardner's column in *Scientific American*. See *http://en.wikipedia.org/wiki/Conway_Game_of_Life* for more information.

The cells in GoL are arranged in a 2D **grid**, either infinite in both directions or wrapped around. A grid wrapped in both directions is called a **torus** because it is topographically equivalent to the surface of a doughnut; see *http://en.wikipedia.org/wiki/Torus*.

Each cell has two states (live and dead) and eight neighbors (north, south, east, west, and the four diagonals). This set of neighbors is sometimes called a Moore neighborhood.

The rules of GoL are **totalistic**, which means that the next state of a cell depends on the number of live neighbors only, not on their arrangement. The following table summarizes the rules:

Number of neighbors	Current state	Next state
2–3	live	live
0–1,4–8	live	dead
3	dead	live
0–2,4–8	dead	dead

This behavior is loosely analogous to real cell growth: cells that are isolated or overcrowded die, but at moderate densities they flourish.

GoL is popular for the following reasons:

- There are simple initial conditions that yield surprisingly complex behavior.
- There are many interesting stable patterns: some oscillate (with various periods), and some move like the spaceships in Wolfram's Rule 110 CA.
- Like Rule 110, GoL is Turing complete.

- Conway posed an intriguing conjecture—that there is no initial condition that yields unbounded growth in the number of live cells—and offered $50 to anyone who could prove or disprove it.
- The increasing availability of computers made it possible to automate the computation and display the results graphically. That turns out to be more fun than Conway's original implementation using a checkerboard.

Implementing Life

To implement GoL efficiently, we can take advantage of the multidimensional convolution function in SciPy. SciPy is a Python package that provides functions related to scientific computing. You can read about it at *http://www.scipy.org/*; if it is not already on your system, you might have to install it.

Convolution is an operation common in digital image processing, where an image is an array of pixels, and many operations involve computing a function of a pixel and its neighbors.

The neighborhood is described by a smaller array called a **kernel** that specifies the location and **weight** of the neighbors. For example, this array:

```
kernel = numpy.array([[1,1,1],
                      [1,0,1],
                      [1,1,1]])
```

represents a neighborhood with eight neighbors, all with weight 1.

Convolution computes the weighted sum of the neighbors for each element of the array. So this kernel computes the sum of the neighbors, not including the center element.

For example, if `array` represents a GoL grid with 1s for live cells and 0s for dead cells, we can use convolution to compute the number of neighbors for each cell:

```
import scipy.ndimage
    neighbors = scipy.ndimage.filters.convolve(array, kernel)
```

Here's an implementation of GoL using `convolve`:

```
import numpy
import scipy.ndimage

class Life(object):

    def __init__(self, n, mode='wrap'):
        self.n = n
        self.mode = mode
        self.array = numpy.random.random_integers(0, 1, (n, n))
        self.weights = numpy.array([[1,1,1],
                                    [1,10,1],
                                    [1,1,1]])
```

```
def step(self):
    con = scipy.ndimage.filters.convolve(self.array,
                                         self.weights,
                                         mode=self.mode)

    boolean = (con==3) | (con==12) | (con==13)
    self.array = numpy.int8(boolean)
```

The attributes of the Life object are n ,the number of rows and columns in the grid; mode, which controls the behaviors of the boundary cells; array, which represents the grid; and weights, which is the kernel used to count the neighbors.

The weight of the center cell is 10, so the number of neighbors is 0-8 for dead cells and 10-18 for live cells.

In step, boolean is a boolean array with True for live cells; numpy.int8 converts it to integers.

To display an animated sequence of grids, I use pyplot. Animation in pyplot is a little awkward, but here's a class that manages it:

```
import matplotlib
matplotlib.use('TkAgg')
import matplotlib.pyplot as pyplot

class LifeViewer(object):

    def __init__(self, life, cmap=matplotlib.cm.gray_r):
        self.life = life
        self.cmap = cmap

        self.fig = pyplot.figure()
        pyplot.axis([0, life.n, 0, life.n])
        pyplot.xticks([])
        pyplot.yticks([])

        self.pcolor = None
        self.update()
```

life is a Life object. cmap is a color map provided by matplotlib; you can see the other color maps at *http://www.scipy.org/Cookbook/Matplotlib/Show_colormaps*.

self.fig is a reference to the matplotlib figure, and self.pcolor is a reference to the **pseudocolor plot** created by update:

```
def update(self):
    if self.pcolor:
        self.pcolor.remove()

    a = self.life.array
    self.pcolor = pyplot.pcolor(a, cmap=self.cmap)
    self.fig.canvas.draw()
```

If there is already a plot, we have to remove it; then we create a new one and invoke draw to update the display.

To run the animation, we need two methods:

```
def animate(self, steps=10):
    self.steps = steps
    self.fig.canvas.manager.window.after(1000, self.animate_callback)
    pyplot.show()

def animate_callback(self):
    for i in range(self.steps):
        self.life.step()
        self.update()
```

animate gets the animation started. It invokes pyplot.show, which sets up the GUI and waits for user events, but *first* it has to invoke window.after to set up a callback, so that animate_callback gets invoked after the window is set up. The first argument is the delay in milliseconds. The second argument is a bound method (see Chapter 19 (*http://greenteapress.com/thinkpython/html/book020.html*) of *Think Python*).

animate_callback invokes step to update the Life object and update to update the display.

Exercise 7-1.

Download my implementation of GoL from *http://thinkcomplex.com/Life.py*.

Start the CA in a random state, and run it until it stabilizes. What stable patterns can you identify?

Life Patterns

If you run GoL from a random starting state, a number of stable patterns are likely to appear. Blocks, boats, beehives, blinkers, and gliders are among the most common.

People have spent embarrassing amounts of time finding and naming these patterns. If you search the web, you will find many collections.

From most initial conditions, GoL quickly reaches a stable state where the number of live cells is nearly constant (usually with a small amount of oscillation).

But there are some simple starting conditions that take a long time to settle down and yield a surprising number of live cells. These patterns are called "Methuselahs" because they are so long-lived.

One of the simplest is the r-pentomino, which has only five cells in the shape of an "r," hence the name. It runs for 1,103 steps and yields 6 gliders, 8 blocks, 4 blinkers, 4 beehives, 1 boat, 1 ship, and 1 loaf. One of the longest-lived small patterns is rabbits, which starts with 9 live cells and takes 17,331 steps to stabilize.

Exercise 7-2.

Start with an r-pentomino as an initial condition, and confirm that the results are consistent with the description above. You might have to adjust the size of the grid and the boundary behavior.

Conway's Conjecture

The existence of long-lived patterns brings us back to Conway's original question: are there initial patterns that never stabilize? Conway thought not, but he described two kinds of patterns that would prove him wrong, a "gun" and a "puffer train." A gun is a stable pattern that periodically produces a spaceship. As the stream of spaceships moves out from the source, the number of live cells grows indefinitely. A puffer train is a translating pattern that leaves live cells in its wake.

It turns out that both of these patterns exist. A team led by Bill Gosper discovered the first, a glider gun now called Gosper's Gun. Gosper also discovered the first puffer train. You can find descriptions and animations of these patterns in several places on the Web.

There are many patterns of both types, but they are not easy to design or find. That is not a coincidence. Conway chose the rules of GoL so that his conjecture would not be obviously true or false. Of all the possible rules for a 2D CA, most yield simple behavior; most initial conditions quickly stabilize or grow unbounded. By avoiding uninteresting CAs, Conway was also avoiding Wolfram's Class 1 and Class 2 behavior, and probably Class 3 as well.

If we believe Wolfram's Principle of Computational Equivalence, we expect GoL to be in Class 4, and it is. The Game of Life was proved Turing complete in 1982 (and again, independently, in 1983). Since then, several people have constructed GoL patterns that implement a Turing machine or another machine known to be Turing complete.

Exercise 7-3.

Many named patterns are available in portable file formats. Modify Life.py to parse one of these formats and initialize the grid.

Realism

Stable patterns in GoL are hard not to notice, especially the ones that move. It is natural to think of them as persistent entities, but remember that a CA is made of cells; there is no such thing as a toad or a loaf. Gliders and other spaceships are even less real because they are not even made up of the same cells over time. So these patterns are like constellations of stars. We perceive them because we are good at seeing patterns or because we have active imaginations, but they are not real.

Right?

Well, not so fast. Many entities that we consider real are also persistent patterns of entities on a smaller scale. Hurricanes are just patterns of air flow, but we give them personal names. And people, like gliders, are not made up of the same cells over time. But even if you replace every cell in your body, we consider you the same person.

This is not a new observation—about 2,500 years ago Heraclitus pointed out that you can't step in the same river twice—but the entities that appear in the Game of Life are a useful test case for thinking about **philosophical realism**.

In the context of philosophy, realism is the view that entities in the world exist independent of human perception and conception. By "perception," I mean the information that we get from our senses, and by "conception," I mean the mental model we form of the world. For example, our vision systems perceive something like a 2D projection of a scene, and our brains use that image to construct a 3D model of the objects in the scene.

Scientific realism pertains to scientific theories and the entities they postulate. A theory postulates an entity if it is expressed in terms of the properties and behavior of the entity. For example, Mendelian genetics postulates a "gene" as a unit that controls a heritable characteristic. Eventually we discovered that genes are encoded in DNA, but for about 50 years, a gene was just a postulated entity. See *http://en.wikipedia.org/wiki/Gene*.

Again, I find it useful to state philosophical positions in a range of strengths, where SR1 is a weak form of scientific realism and SR4 is a strong form:

SR1
> Scientific theories are true or false to the degree that they approximate reality, but no theory is exactly true. Some postulated entities may be real, but there is no principled way to say which ones.

SR2
> As science advances, our theories become better approximations of reality. At least some postulated entities are known to be real.

SR3
> Some theories are exactly true; others are approximately true. Entities postulated by true theories, and some entities in approximate theories, are real.

SR4
> A theory is true if it describes reality correctly, and false otherwise. The entities postulated by true theories are real; others are not.

SR4 is so strong that it is probably untenable; by such a strict criterion, almost all current theories are known to be false. Most realists would accept something in the space between SR1 and SR3.

Instrumentalism

SR1 is so weak that it verges on **instrumentalism**, which is the view that we can't say whether a theory is true or false because we can't know whether a theory corresponds to reality. Theories are instruments that we use for our purposes; a theory is useful (or not) to the degree that it is fit for its purpose.

To see whether you are comfortable with instrumentalism, consider the following statements:

> "Entities in the Game of Life aren't real; they are just patterns of cells that people have given cute names."

> "A hurricane is just a pattern of air flow, but it is a useful description because it allows us to make predictions and communicate about the weather."

> "Freudian entities like the id and the superego aren't real, but they are useful tools for thinking and communicating about psychology (or at least some people think so)."

> "Electrons are postulated entities in our best theories of electromagnetism, but they aren't real. We could construct other theories, without postulating electrons, that would be just as useful."

> "Many of the things in the world that we identify as objects are arbitrary collections like constellations. For example, a mushroom is just the fruiting body of a fungus, most of which grows underground as a barely-contiguous network of cells. We focus on mushrooms for practical reasons like visibility and edibility."

> "Some objects have sharp boundaries, but many are fuzzy. For example, which molecules are part of your body: air in your lungs? Food in your stomach? Nutrients in your blood? Nutrients in a cell? Water in a cell? Structural parts of a cell? Hair? Dead skin? Dirt? Bacteria on your skin? Bacteria in your gut? Mitochondria? How many of those molecules do you include when you weigh yourself? Conceiving of the world in terms of discrete objects is useful, but the entities we identify are not real."

Give yourself one point for each statement you agree with. If you score 4 or more, you might be an instrumentalist!

If you are more comfortable with some of these statements than others, ask yourself why. What are the differences in these scenarios that influence your reaction? Can you make a principled distinction between them?

Exercise 7-4.

Read *http://en.wikipedia.org/wiki/Instrumentalism* and construct a sequence of statements that characterize instrumentalism in a range of strengths.

Turmites

If you generalize the Turing machine to two dimensions or add a read-write head to a 2D CA, the result is a cellular automaton called a turmite. It is named after a termite because of the way the read-write head moves, but spelled wrong as an homage to Alan Turing.

The most famous turmite is Langton's ant, discovered by Chris Langton in 1986. See *http://en.wikipedia.org/wiki/Langton_ant*.

The ant is a read-write head with four states, which you can think of as facing north, south, east, or west. The cells have two states, black and white.

The rules are simple. During each time step, the ant checks the color of the cell it is on. If it is black, the ant turns to the right, changes the cell to white, and moves forward one space. If the cell is white, the ant turns left, changes the cell to black, and moves forward.

Given a simple world, a simple set of rules, and only one moving part, you might expect to see simple behavior—but you should know better by now. Starting with all white cells, Langton's ant moves in a seemingly random pattern for more than 10,000 steps before it enters a cycle with a period of 104 steps. After each cycle, the ant is translated diagonally, so it leaves a trail called the "highway."

If you start with multiple turmites, they interact with each other in seemingly complex ways. If one turmite is on the highway, another can follow it, overtake it, and cause it to reverse its pattern, moving back up the highway and leaving only white cells behind.

Exercise 7-5.

Write an implementation of Langton's ant.

You can find a solution in `TurmiteWorld.py`, which is part of Swampy. See *http://think python.com/swampy/*.

CHAPTER 8

Fractals

To understand fractals, we have to start with dimensions. The dimension of a space is the number of coordinates we need to specify a point in a space. A number line takes one coordinate, a Euclidean plane takes two, a solid takes three, and so on. See *http://en.wikipedia.org/wiki/Dimension*.

For simple geometric objects, dimension is defined in terms of scaling behavior; that is, how size depends on length, l. For example, the area of a square is l^2; the exponent, 2, indicates that a square is two-dimensional. Similarly, the volume of a cube is l^3, and a cube is three-dimensional. A line has dimension 1, and if we think of a point as infinitesimally small, it has dimension 0.

Fractal dimension is a more precise and more general extension of this definition. There are several versions; the one I find easiest to understand and apply is the **box-counting dimension**, which is defined for a set, S, of points in a d-dimensional space. See *http://en.wikipedia.org/wiki/Box-counting_dimension*.

To compute the box-counting dimension, we divide the space into a grid where the size of each cell is ε. Then we count $N(\varepsilon)$, the number of cells that contain at least one element of S. As ε gets smaller, $N(\varepsilon)$ gets bigger. For many objects the relationship has the following form:

$$N(\varepsilon) \sim (1 / \varepsilon)^D$$

The box-counting dimension, D_{box}, is defined to be the exponent, D. Taking the log of both sides and rearranging yields:

$$D_{box} = \frac{\log N(\varepsilon)}{\log(1/\varepsilon)}$$

More formally, D_{box} is the limit of this ratio as ε goes to zero.

Fractal CAs

To investigate the behavior of the fractal dimension, we'll apply it to cellular automata. Box counting for CAs is simple; we just count the number of "on" cells in each time step and add them up.

As an example, consider Rule 254. Figure 8-1 shows what it looks like after $t = 4$ time steps, and Figure 8-2 shows what it looks like after $t = 8$ time steps.

Figure 8-1. Rule 254 after 4 time steps

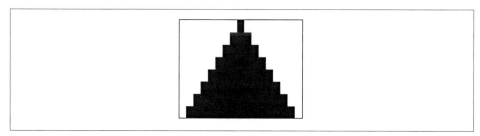

Figure 8-2. Rule 254 after 8 time steps

As t increases, we can imagine the triangle getting bigger, but for purposes of box counting, it makes more sense to imagine the cells getting smaller. In that case, the size of the cells, ε, is just $1/t$.

After one time step, there is one black cell. After 2 time steps, there are a total of 4, then 9, then 16, then 25. As expected, the area of the triangle goes up quadratically. More formally, $N(\varepsilon) = (1/\varepsilon)^2$, so $D_{box} = 2$. We conclude that a triangle is two-dimensional.

Rule 18 is more interesting. Figure 8-3 shows what it looks like after 64 steps, and Figure 8-4 shows $N(\varepsilon)$ versus $1/\varepsilon$ on a log-log scale.

To estimate D_{box}, I fit a line to this curve; its slope is 1.56. D_{box} is a non-integer, which means that this set of points is a **fractal**. As t increases, the slope approaches $log3/log2$, which is the fractal dimension of Sierpiński's triangle. See *http://en.wikipedia.org/wiki/Sierpinski_triangle*.

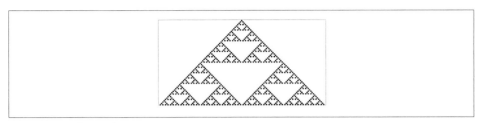

Figure 8-3. Rule 18 after 64 time steps

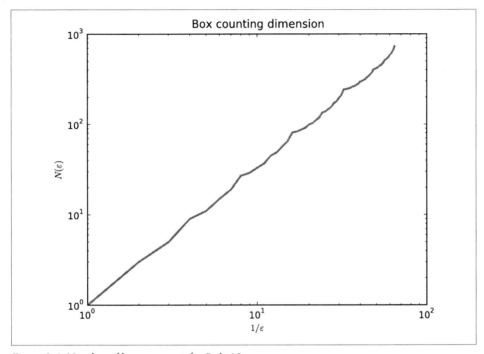

Figure 8-4. Number of boxes versus t for Rule 18

Exercise 8-1.

Write a function that takes a CA object; plots $N(\varepsilon)$ versus $1/\varepsilon$, where $\varepsilon = 1/t$; and estimates D_{box}.

Can you find other CAs with non-integer fractal dimensions? Be careful, you might have to run the CA for a while before D_{box} converges.

Here are some functions from numpy you might find useful: cumsum, log, and polyfit.

You can download my solution from *http://thinkcomplex.com/fractal.py*.

Exercise 8-2.

In 1990, Bak, Chen, and Tang proposed a cellular automaton that is an abstract model of a forest fire. Each cell is in one of three states: empty, occupied by a tree, or on fire.

The rules of the CA are the following:

1. An empty cell becomes occupied with probability p.
2. A cell with a tree burns if any of its neighbors is on fire.
3. A cell with a tree spontaneously burns with probability f, even if none of its neighbors is on fire.
4. A cell with a burning tree becomes an empty cell in the next time step.

Read about this model at *http://en.wikipedia.org/wiki/Forest-fire_model*, and write a program that implements it. You might want to start with a copy of *http://thinkcomplex.com/Life.py*.

Starting from a random initial condition, run the CA until it reaches a steady state where the number of trees no longer increases or decreases consistently. You might have to tune p and f.

In a steady state, is the geometry of the forest fractal? What is its fractal dimension?

Percolation

Many of the CAs we have seen so far are not physical models; that is, they are not intended to describe systems in the real world. But some CAs are designed explicitly as physical models. In this section, we consider a simple grid-based model of percolation; in the next chapter, we see examples that model forest fires, avalanches, and earthquakes.

Percolation is a process in which a fluid flows through a semiporous material. Examples include oil in rock formations, water in paper, and hydrogen gas in micropores. Percolation models are also used to study systems that are not literally percolation, including epidemics and networks of electrical resistors; see *http://en.wikipedia.org/wiki/Percolation_theory*.

Percolation processes often exhibit a phase change; that is, an abrupt transition from one behavior (low flow) to another (high flow) with a small change in a continuous parameter (like the porosity of the material). This transition is sometimes called a "tipping point."

There are two common models of these systems: bond percolation and site percolation. Bond percolation is based on a grid of sites where each site is connected to four neighbors by a bond. Each bond is either porous or non-porous. A set of sites that are connected (directly or indirectly) by porous bonds is called a cluster. In the vocabulary of graphs, a site is a vertex, a bond is an edge, and a cluster is a connected subgraph.

Site percolation is based on a grid of cells where each cell represents a porous segment of the material or a non-porous segment. If two porous cells are adjacent, they are considered connected; a set of connected cells is considered a cluster.

The rate of flow in a percolation system is primarily determined by whether or not the porous cells form a path all the way through the material, so it is useful to know whether a set of cells (or bonds) contains a "spanning cluster." There are several definitions of a spanning cluster; the choice depends on the system you are trying to model. The simplest choice is a cluster that reaches the top and bottom row of the grid.

To model the porosity of the material, it is common to define a parameter, p, of the probability that any cell (or bond) is porous. For a given value of p, you can estimate $R(p)$—which is the probability that there is a spanning cluster—by generating a large number of random grids and computing the fraction that contain a spanning cluster. This way of estimating probabilities is called a Monte Carlo simulation because it a similar to a game of chance.

Percolation models are often used to compute a critical value, p_c, which is the fraction of porous segments where the phase change occurs; that is, where the probability of a spanning cluster increases quickly from near 0 to near 1.

Exercise 8-3.

The paper "Efficient Monte Carlo Algorithm and High-Precision Results for Percolation," by Newman and Ziff, presents an efficient algorithm for checking whether there is a path through a grid. You can download this paper from *http://arxiv.org/abs/cond -mat/0005264*. Read the paper, implement their algorithm, and see if you can reproduce their Figure 2(a).

1. What is the difference between what Newman and Ziff call the "microcanonical ensemble" and the "canonical ensemble"? You might find it useful to read about the use of these terms in statistical mechanics at *http://en.wikipedia.org/wiki/Statis tical_mechanics*. Which one is easier to estimate by Monte Carlo simulation?

2. What algorithm do they use to merge two clusters efficiently?

3. What is the primary reason their algorithm is faster than the simpler alternative?

CHAPTER 9

Self-Organized Criticality

Sand Piles

In 1987, Bak, Tang, and Wiesenfeld published a paper in *Physical Review Letters*, "Self-organized criticality: An explanation of $1/f$ noise." You can download it from *http://prl .aps.org/abstract/PRL/v59/i4/p381_1*.

The title takes some explaining. A system is critical if it is in transition between two phases; for example, water at its freezing point is a critical system.

A variety of critical systems demonstrate common behaviors:

- Long-tailed distributions of some physical quantities: for example, in freezing water, the distribution of crystal sizes is characterized by a power law.

- Fractal geometries: freezing water tends to form fractal patterns—the canonical example is a snowflake. Fractals are characterized by self-similarity; that is, parts of the pattern resemble scaled copies of the whole.

- Variations in time that exhibit pink noise: what we call "noise" is a time series with many frequency components. In white noise, all of the components have equal power. In pink noise, low-frequency components have more power than high-frequency components. Specifically, the power at frequency f is proportional to $1/f$. Visible light with this power spectrum looks pink, hence the name.

Critical systems are usually unstable. For example, to keep water in a partially frozen state requires active control of the temperature. If the system is near the critical temperature, a small deviation tends to move the system into one phase or the other.

Many natural systems exhibit characteristic behaviors of criticality, but if critical points are unstable, they should not be common in nature. This is the puzzle Bak, Tang, and Wiesenfeld address. Their solution is called self-organized criticality (SOC), where "self-organized" means that from any initial condition, the system tends to move toward a critical state (and stay there) without external control.

As an example, they propose a model of a sand pile. The model is not realistic, but it has become the standard example of self-organized criticality.

The model is a 2D cellular automaton where the state of each cell, $z(i, j)$, represents the slope of a part of a sand pile. During each time step, each cell is checked to see whether it exceeds some critical value, K. If so, an "avalanche" occurs that transfers sand to neighboring cells; specifically, $z(i, j)$ is decreased by 4, and each of the 4 neighbors is increased by 1.

At the perimeter of the grid, all cells are kept at $z = 0$, so the excess spills over the edge. To initialize the system, Bak et al. start with all $z > K$ and evolve the system until it stabilizes. Then they observe the effect of small perturbations; they choose a cell at random, increment its value by 1, and evolve the system again, until it stabilizes.

For each perturbation, they measure D, the total number of cells that are affected by the resulting avalanche. Most of the time, D is small, usually 1. But occasionally a large avalanche affects a substantial fraction of the grid. The distribution of D turns out to be long-tailed, which supports the claim that the system is in a critical state.

Exercise 9-1.

Read the paper and write a program that implements their CA. You might want to start with a copy of *http://thinkcomplex.com/Life.py*.

See if you can reproduce their Figure 2(a), which shows the distribution of cluster sizes.

After the system has been running for a while, compute its fractal dimension.

Spectral Density

To understand $1/f$ noise, we have to take a detour to understand spectral density. If $h(t)$ is a signal that varies in time, it can be described by its power spectral density, $P(f)$, which is a function that maps from a frequency, f, to the amount of power the signal contains at that frequency.

This analysis applies to any varying signal, but I use sound as an example. The note we call "middle A" corresponds to a frequency of 440 cycles per second, or Hertz (Hz). If you strike a middle A tuning fork, it produces a sound that is close to a pure sine wave at 440 Hz. But if you play the same note on a piano, what you hear is a complex sound that contains components at many different frequencies. The frequency with the most power is 440, which is why we perceive the sound as a middle A, but there are also components at 880, 1320, and many higher frequencies. These components are called harmonics.

What we identify as the pitch of a sound is usually the dominant frequency component. But if a sound contains many different components with roughly the same power, it has no particular pitch. To our ears, it sounds like noise.

Spectral analysis is the process of taking a signal and computing its spectral density.[1] The first step is to compute the Fourier transform of $h(t)$:

$$H(\omega) = \int_{-\infty}^{\infty} h(t)e^{i\omega t}dt$$

where $\omega = 2\pi f$ is the angular frequency in radians per second (rather than cycles per second). The advantage of working with angular frequency is that it reduces the number of times the term 2π appears.

$H(\omega)$ is written with a capital letter because it is a complex number, which you can think of as a vector with a magnitude, $|H(\omega)|$, and an angle. The power spectral density is related to the Fourier transform by the following relation:

$$P(f) = |H(2\pi f)|^2$$

Depending on the application, we may not care about the difference between f and $-f$. In that case, we would use the one-sided power spectral density:

$$P(f) = |H(2\pi f)|^2 + |H(-2\pi f)|^2$$

So far we have assumed that $h(t)$ is a continuous function, but often it is a series of values at discrete times. In that case, we can replace the continuous Fourier transform with the discrete Fourier transform (DFT). Suppose that we have N values h_k with k in the range from 0 to $N-1$. The DFT is written H_n, where n is an index related to frequency:

$$H_n = \sum_{k=0}^{N-1} h_k e^{2\pi i k n / N} \qquad \text{9.1}$$

Each element of this sequence corresponds to a particular frequency. If the elements of h_k are equally spaced in time, with time step d, the frequency that corresponds to H_n is:

$$f_n = \frac{n}{Nd}$$

To get the one-sided power spectral density, you can compute H_n with n in the range $-N/2$ to $N/2$, and:

$$P_n = |H_n|^2 + |H_{-n}|^2$$

1. The presentation here follows Press et al, *Numerical Recipes in C.*

To avoid negative indices, it is conventional to compute H_n with n in the range 0 to $N-1$, and use the relation $H_{-n} = H_{N-n}$ to convert.

Exercise 9-2.

Write a function named `dft` that takes h, a sequence of N values, and returns the sequence H_n with n in the range 0 to $N-1$.

Python provides support for complex numbers as a built-in type. The function `complex` takes two arguments, a real part and an imaginary part, and returns a complex number:

```
>>> complex(1, 1)
(1+1j)
```

The `cmath` module provides math functions that support complex numbers:

```
>>> import cmath
>>> i = complex(0, 1)
>>> N = 128
>>> cmath.exp(2 * math.pi * i / N)
(0.99879545620517241+0.049067674327418015j)
```

What is the order of growth runtime of `dft`?

Hoisting is a way to speed up code by moving an expression that does not change out of a loop. See *http://en.wikipedia.org/wiki/Loop-invariant_code_motion*. You can make your code easier to read and more efficient by hoisting:

$$W = e^{2\pi i / N}$$

What effect does hoisting have on the order of growth?

Fast Fourier Transform

The Fast Fourier Transform (FFT) is an efficient algorithm for computing the DFT. It is often attributed to Cooley and Tukey, but it was independently discovered several times earlier. See *http://en.wikipedia.org/wiki/Fast_Fourier_transform*.

The first step toward the FFT is to rewrite the equation above with the substitution $W = e^{2\pi i / N}$:

$$H_n = \sum_{k=0}^{N-1} h_k W^{nk}$$

The second step is the Danielson-Lanczos Lemma, which states:

$$H_n = H_n^e + W^k H_n^o$$

where H^e is the DFT of the even-indexed elements of h, and H^o is the DFT of the odd-indexed elements. This lemma follows naturally from the definition of H_n; you can see a proof at *http://mathworld.wolfram.com/Danielson-LanczosLemma.html*.

This lemma suggests a recursive algorithm for evaluating the DFT of a sequence h. If h has only a single element, then $H = h$. Otherwise,

1. Split h into h^e and h^o.
2. Compute H^e and H^o by making two recursive calls.
3. Use the lemma to combine H^e and H^o to form H.

If H has $2N$ elements, H^e and H^o have only N. In order to merge them, you have to wrap around, but you can do that because $H^e_{n+N} = H^e_n$.

This recursive algorithm is the Fast Fourier Transform.

Exercise 9-3.

Write a function called `fft` that implements the Fast Fourier Transform. To check your function, you can compare it to the function `fft` provided by the module `numpy.fft`.

What is the order of growth runtime of your implementation? What is the order of growth for the space required?

Most FFT implementations use a clever indexing scheme to avoid copying the sequence; instead, they transform the elements in place. You can read *http://en.wikipedia.org/wiki/Butterfly_diagram* to get the details.

Once your `fft` is working, write a function named `psd` that takes a sequence, h, and returns its one-sided power spectral density, P.

You can download my solution from *http://thinkcomplex.com/Fourier.py*.

Pink Noise

In a follow-up paper in 1988, Bak, Tang, and Wiesenfeld looked at a time series $F(t)$, which is the number of cells that exceed the threshold during each time step. If I understand their model, they seed avalanches by incrementing the state of a random cell at random intervals; for example, there might be a fixed probability during each time step that a cell is incremented. In this model (unlike the previous one), there may be more than one avalanche at a time.

A plot of $F(t)$ shows that it is noisy but not completely random, which is consistent with pink, or $1/f$ noise. As a stronger test, they plot the power spectral density of F on a log-log scale. If F is $1/f$ noise, then:

$$P_n \sim 1/f_n = \frac{Nd}{n}$$

Since the units of time in this model are arbitrary, we can choose $d = 1$. Taking the log of both sides yields:

$$\log P_n \sim \log N - \log n$$

So on a log-log scale, the PSD of $1/f$ noise is a straight line with slope -1.

Exercise 9-4.

Modify your implementation of the sand pile model to increment a random cell at random intervals, and record the number of cells that exceed the threshold during each time step.

To estimate the average PSD, you can divide the time series into chunks of 128 to 256 values, compute the PSD of each chunk, and average together the PSDs. Plot the result on a log-log scale and estimate the slope.

Exercise 9-5.

In a 1989 paper, "Self-organized criticality in the 'Game of Life'," Bak, Chen, and Creutz present evidence that the Game of Life is a self-organized critical system (*http://www .nature.com/nature/journal/v342/n6251/abs/342780a0.html*).

To replicate their tests, run the GoL CA until it stabilizes, then choose a random cell and toggle it. Run the CA until it stabilizes again, keeping track of t, the number of time steps it takes, and s, the number of cells affected. Repeat for a large number of trials, and plot the distributions of t and s. Also, see if you can think of an effective experiment to test for $1/f$ noise.

Some later work has called the conclusions of this paper into question. You might want to read Blok, "Life without bounds," at *http://ubc.academia.edu/RikBlok/Papers/ 1228444*.

Reductionism and Holism

The original paper by Bak, Tang, and Wiesenfeld is one of the most frequently cited papers in the last few decades. Many new systems have been shown to be self-organized critical, and the sand pile model in particular has been studied in detail.

As it turns out, the sand pile model is not a very good model of a sand pile. Sand is dense and not very sticky, so momentum has a non-negligible effect on the behavior of avalanches. As a result, there are fewer very large and very small avalanches than the model predicts, and the distribution is not long tailed.

Bak has suggested that this observation misses the point. The sand pile model is not meant to be a realistic model of a sand pile; it is meant to be a simple example of a broad category of models.

To understand this point, it is useful to think about two kinds of models, **reductionist** and **holistic**. A reductionist model describes a system by describing its parts and their interactions. When a reductionist model is used as an explanation, it depends on an analogy between the components of the model and the components of the system.

For example, to explain why the ideal gas law holds, we can model the molecules that make up a gas with point masses and model their interactions as elastic collisions. If you simulate or analyze this model, you find that it obeys the ideal gas law. This model is satisfactory to the degree that molecules in a gas behave like molecules in the model. The analogy is between the parts of the system and the parts of the model.

Holistic models are more focused on similarities between systems and less interested in analogous parts. A holistic approach to modeling often consists of two steps, not necessarily in this order:

- Identify a kind of behavior that appears in a variety of systems.
- Find the simplest model that demonstrates that behavior.

For example, in *The Selfish Gene*, Richard Dawkins suggests that genetic evolution is just one example of an evolutionary system. He identifies the essential elements of the category—discrete replicators, variability, and differential reproduction—and proposes that any system that has these elements displays similar behavior, including complexity without design.

As another example of an evolutionary system, he proposes **memes**, which are thoughts or behaviors that are "replicated" by transmission from person to person. As memes compete for the resource of human attention, they evolve in ways that are similar to genetic evolution.

Critics of memetics have pointed out that memes are a poor analogy for genes. Memes differ from genes in many obvious ways, but Dawkins has argued that these differences are beside the point because memes are not *supposed* to be analogous to genes. Rather, memetics and genetics are examples of the same category: evolutionary systems. The differences between them emphasize the real point, which is that evolution is a general model that applies to many seemingly disparate systems. The logical structure of this argument is shown in Figure 9-1.

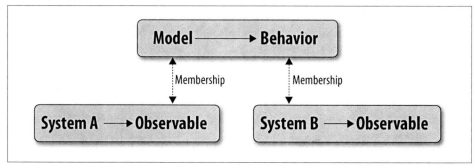

Figure 9-1. The logical structure of a holistic model

Bak has made a similar argument that self-organized criticality is a general model for a broad category of systems. According to Wikipedia, "SOC is typically observed in slowly-driven non-equilibrium systems with extended degrees of freedom and a high level of nonlinearity."

Many natural systems demonstrate behaviors characteristic of critical systems. Bak's explanation for this prevalence is that these systems are examples of the broad category of self-organized criticality. There are two ways to support this argument. One is to build a realistic model of a particular system and show that the model exhibits SOC. The second is to show that SOC is a feature of many diverse models and to identify the essential characteristics those models have in common.

The first approach, which I characterize as reductionist, can explain the behavior of a particular system. The second, a holistic approach, explains the prevalence of criticality in natural systems. They are different models with different purposes.

For reductionist models, realism is the primary virtue, and simplicity is secondary. For holistic models, it is the other way around.

Exercise 9-6.

Read *http://en.wikipedia.org/wiki/Reductionism* and *http://en.wikipedia.org/wiki/Holism*.

Exercise 9-7.

In a 1996 paper in *Nature*, Frette et al report the results of experiments with rice piles (*http://www.nature.com/nature/journal/v379/n6560/abs/379049a0.html*). They find that some kinds of rice yield evidence of critical behavior, but others do not.

Similarly, Pruessner and Jensen studied large-scale versions of the forest fire model (using an algorithm similar to Newman and Ziff's). In their 2004 paper, "Efficient algorithm for the forest fire model," they present evidence that the system is not critical after all (*http://pre.aps.org/abstract/PRE/v70/i6/e066707*).

How do these results bear on Bak's claim that SOC explains the prevalence of critical phenomena in nature?

Exercise 9-8.

In *The Fractal Geometry of Nature*, Benoit Mandelbrot proposes what he calls a "heretical" explanation for the prevalence of long-tailed distributions in natural systems (page 344). It may not be, as Bak suggests, that many systems can generate this behavior in isolation. Instead there may be only a few, but there may be interactions between systems that cause the behavior to propagate.

To support this argument, Mandelbrot points out the following:

- The distribution of observed data is often "the joint effect of a fixed underlying 'true distribution' and a highly variable 'filter.'"
- Long-tailed distributions are robust to filtering; that is, "a wide variety of filters leave their asymptotic behavior unchanged."

What do you think of this argument? Would you characterize it as reductionist or holistic?

SOC, Causation, and Prediction

If a stock market index drops by a fraction of a percent in a day, there is no need for an explanation. But if it drops 10%, people want to know why. Pundits on television are willing to offer explanations, but the real answer may be that there is no explanation.

Day-to-day variability in the stock market shows evidence of criticality: the distribution of value changes is long-tailed, and the time series exhibits $1/f$ noise. If the stock market is a self-organized critical system, we should expect occasional large changes as part of the ordinary behavior of the market.

The distribution of earthquake sizes is also long-tailed, and there are simple models of the dynamics of geological faults that might explain this behavior. If these models are right, they imply that large earthquakes are unexceptional; that is, they do not require explanation any more than small earthquakes do.

Similarly, Charles Perrow has suggested that failures in large engineered systems, like nuclear power plants, are like avalanches in the sand pile model. Most failures are small, isolated, and harmless, but occasionally a coincidence of bad fortune yields a catastrophe. When big accidents occur, investigators go looking for the cause, but if Perrow's normal accident theory is correct, there may be no cause.

These conclusions are not comforting. Among other things, they imply that large earthquakes and some kinds of accidents are fundamentally unpredictable. It is impossible to look at the state of a critical system and say whether a large avalanche is "due." If the system is in a critical state, then a large avalanche is always possible. It just depends on the next grain of sand.

In a sand pile model, what is the cause of a large avalanche? Philosophers sometimes distinguish the **proximate** cause, which is most immediately responsible, from the **ultimate** cause, which is, for whatever reason, considered the true cause.

In the sand pile model, the proximate cause of an avalanche is a grain of sand, but the grain that causes a large avalanche is identical to any other grain, so it offers no special explanation. The ultimate cause of a large avalanche is the structure and dynamics of the systems as a whole: large avalanches occur because they are a property of the system.

Many social phenomena, including wars, revolutions, epidemics, inventions, and terrorist attacks, are characterized by long-tailed distributions. If the reason for these distributions is that social systems are critical, that suggests that major historical events may be fundamentally unpredictable and unexplainable.

Exercise 9-9.

Read about the Great Man theory of history at *http://en.wikipedia.org/wiki/Great_man_theory*. What implication does self-organized criticality have for this theory?

CHAPTER 10

Agent-Based Models

Thomas Schelling

In 1971, Thomas Schelling published "Dynamic Models of Segregation," which proposes a simple model of racial segregation. The Schelling model of the world is a grid; each cell represents a house. The houses are occupied by two kinds of "agents," labeled red and blue, in roughly equal numbers. About 10% of the houses are empty.

At any point in time, an agent might be happy or unhappy, depending on the other agents in the neighborhood. The neighborhood of each house is the set of eight adjacent cells. In one version of the model, agents are happy if they have at least two neighbors like themselves and unhappy if they have one or zero.

The simulation proceeds by choosing an agent at random and checking to see whether it is happy. If so, then nothing happens; if not, the agent chooses one of the unoccupied cells at random and moves.

You might not be surprised to hear that this model leads to some segregation, but you might be surprised by the degree. Fairly quickly, clusters of similar agents appear. The clusters grow and coalesce over time until there are a small number of large clusters and most agents live in homogeneous neighborhoods.

If you did not know the process and only saw the result, you might assume that the agents were racist, but in fact all of them would be perfectly happy in a mixed neighborhood. Since they prefer not to be greatly outnumbered, they might be considered xenophobic at worst. Of course, these agents are a wild simplification of real people, so it may not be appropriate to apply these descriptions at all.

Racism is a complex human problem; it is hard to imagine that such a simple model could shed light on it. But in fact it provides a strong argument about the relationship between a system and its parts: if you observe segregation in a real city, you cannot conclude that individual racism is the immediate cause, or even that the people in the city are racists.

But we have to keep in mind the limitations of this argument: Schelling's model demonstrates a possible cause of segregation but says nothing about actual causes.

Exercise 10-1.

Implement Schelling's model in a grid. From random initial conditions, how does the system evolve?

Define a statistic that measures the degree of segregation, and plot this statistic over time.

Experiment with the parameters of the model. What happens as the agents become more tolerant? What happens if the agents are only happy in mixed neighborhoods; that is, if they are unhappy if too many of their neighbors are like themselves?

Exercise 10-2.

In the recent book *The Big Sort*, Bill Bishop argues that American society is increasingly segregated by political opinion, as people choose to live among like-minded neighbors.

The mechanism Bishop hypothesizes is not that people, like the agents in Schelling's model, are more likely to move if they are isolated but that when they move for any reason, they are likely to choose a neighborhood with people like themselves.

Modify your implementation of Schelling's model to simulate this kind of behavior and see if it yields similar degrees of segregation.

Agent-Based Models

Schelling's model is one of the first and most famous agent-based models. Since the 1970s, agent-based modeling has become an important tool in economics and other social sciences, and in some natural sciences.

The characteristics of agent-based models include:

- Agents that model intelligent behavior, usually with a simple set of rules.
- Agents that are usually situated in space (or in a network) and interact with each other locally.
- Agents that usually have imperfect, local information.
- Variability between agents in most cases.
- Random elements in most cases, either among the agents or in the world.

Agent-based models are useful for modeling the dynamics of systems that are not in equilibrium (although they are also used to study equilibrium). They are particularly useful for understanding relationships between individual decisions and system behavior, or as in the title of Schelling's book, *Micromotives and Macrobehavior*.

For more about agent-based modeling, see *http://en.wikipedia.org/wiki/Agent-based _model*.

Traffic Jams

What causes traffic jams? In some cases, there is an obvious cause like an accident, a speed trap, or something else that disturbs the flow of traffic. But other times traffic jams appear for no apparent reason.

Agent-based models can help explain spontaneous traffic jams. As an example, I implemented a simple highway simulation based on a model in Resnick's *Turtles, Termites, and Traffic Jams*.

You can download my program from *http://thinkcomplex.com/Highway.py*. It uses TurtleWorld, which is part of Swampy. See *http://thinkpython.com/swampy*.

This module defines two classes: Highway, which inherits from TurtleWorld, and Driver, which inherits from Turtle.

The Highway is a one-lane road that forms a circle, but it is displayed as a series of rows that spiral down the canvas. Each Driver starts with a random position and speed. At each time step, each Driver accelerates or brakes based on the distance between it and the Driver in front. Here is an example:

```
def choose_acceleration(self, dist):
    if dist < self.safe_distance:
        return -1
    else:
        return 0.3
```

If the following distance is too short, the Driver brakes; otherwise, it accelerates. In addition, if the current speed would cause a collision, the Driver comes to a complete stop. Also, there is a speed limit for each driver.

If you run Highway.py, you will probably see a traffic jam, and the natural question is, "why?" There is nothing about the Highway or Driver behavior that obviously causes traffic jams.

Exercise 10-3.

Experiment with the parameters of the system to identify the factors that are necessary and sufficient to cause traffic jams. Some of the factors to explore are:

Density
> What happens as the number of drivers (or the length of the highway) increases?

Acceleration and braking
> What happens if drivers accelerate faster or brake more gently?

Safe distance
> What happens as the safe distance between drivers changes?

Heterogeneity
> What if all drivers are not the same; for example, what if they have different speed limits or following distances?

Boids

In 1987, Craig Reynolds published "Flocks, herds, and schools: A distributed behavioral model," which describes an agent-based model of herd behavior. You can download his paper from *http://www.red3d.com/cwr/papers/1987/boids.html*.

Agents in this models are called "boids," which is both a contraction of "bird-oid" and an accented pronunciation of "bird" (although boids are also used to model fish and herding land animals). Each agent simulates three behaviors:

Collision avoidance
    Avoid obstacles, including other birds.

Flock centering
    Move toward the center of the flock.

Velocity matching
    Align velocity with neighboring birds.

Boids make decisions based on local information only; each boid only sees (or pays attention to) other boids in its field of vision and range.

The Visual package, also known as VPython, is well suited for implementing boids. It provides simple 3D graphics as well as vector objects and operations that are useful for the computations.

You can download my implementation from *http://thinkcomplex.com/Boids.py*. It is based in part on the description of boids in Flake's *The Computational Beauty of Nature*.

The program defines two classes: Boid, which implements the boid algorithm, and World, which contains a list of boids and a "carrot" the boids are attracted to.

The boid algorithm uses get_neighbors to find other boids in the field of view:

```
def get_neighbors(self, others, radius, angle):
    boids = []
    for other in others:
        if other is self:
            continue

        offset = other.pos - self.pos

        # if not in range, skip it
        if offset.mag > radius:
            continue

        # if not within viewing angle, skip it
        if self.vel.diff_angle(offset) > angle:
            continue

        # otherwise add it to the list
        boids.append(other)

    return boids
```

get_neighbors uses vector subtraction to compute the vector from self to other. The magnitude of this vector is the distance to the other boid. diff_angle computes the angle between the velocity of self, which is also the line of sight, and the other boid.

center finds the center of mass of the boids in the field of view and returns a vector pointing toward it:

```
def center(self, others):
        close = self.get_neighbors(others, r_center, a_center)
        t = [other.pos for other in close]
        if t:
            center = sum(t)/len(t)
            toward = vector(center - self.pos)
            return limit_vector(toward)
        else:
            return null_vector
```

Similarly, avoid finds the center of mass of any obstacles in range and returns a vector pointing away from it, copy returns the difference between the current heading and the average heading of the neighbors, and love computes the heading toward the carrot.

set_goal computes the weighed sum of these goals, and sets the overall goal:

```
def set_goal(self, boids, carrot):
        self.goal = (w_avoid * self.avoid(boids, carrot) +
                     w_center * self.center(boids) +
                     w_copy * self.copy(boids) +
                     w_love * self.love(carrot))
```

Finally, move updates the velocity, position, and attitude of the boid:

```
def move(self, mu=0.1):
        self.vel = (1-mu) * self.vel + mu * self.goal
        self.vel.mag = 1

        self.pos += dt * self.vel
        self.axis = b_length * self.vel.norm()
```

The new velocity is the weighted sum of the old velocity and the goal. The parameter mu determines how quickly the boids can change speed and direction. The time step dt determines how far the boids move.

Many parameters influence flock behavior, including the range, angle, and weight for each behavior, and the maneuverability, mu.

These parameters determine the ability of the boids to form and maintain a flock, and the patterns of motion and organization in the flock. For some settings, the boids resemble a flock of birds; other settings resemble a school of fish or a cloud of flying insects.

Exercise 10-4.

Run my implementation of the boid algorithm, and experiment with different parameters. What happens if you "turn off" one of the behaviors by setting the weight to 0?

To generate more bird-like behavior, Flake suggests adding a fourth behavior to maintain a clear line of sight; in other words, if there is another boid directly ahead, the boid should move away laterally. What effect do you expect this rule to have on the behavior of the flock? Implement it and see.

Prisoner's Dilemma

The Prisoner's Dilemma is a topic of study in game theory, so it's not the fun kind of game. Instead, it is the kind of game that sheds light on human motivation and behavior.

Here is the presentation of the dilemma from *http://en.wikipedia.org/wiki/Prisoner's _dilemma*.

> Two suspects [Alice and Bob] are arrested by the police. The police have insufficient evidence for a conviction, and, having separated the prisoners, visit each of them to offer the same deal. If one testifies against the other (defects) and the other remains silent (cooperates), the defector goes free and the silent accomplice receives the full one-year sentence. If both remain silent, both prisoners are sentenced to only one month in jail for a minor charge. If each betrays the other, each receives a three-month sentence. Each prisoner must choose to betray the other or to remain silent. Each one is assured that the other would not know about the betrayal before the end of the investigation. How should the prisoners act?

Notice that in this context, "cooperate" means to keep silent, not to cooperate with police.

It is tempting to say that the players should cooperate with each other since they would both be better off. But neither player knows what the other will do. Looking at it from Bob's point of view:

- If Alice remains silent, Bob is better off defecting.
- If Alice defects, Bob is better off defecting.

Either way, Bob is better off defecting. From her point of view, Alice reaches the same conclusion. So if both players do the math, and no other factors come into play, we expect them to defect and be worse off for it.

This result is saddening because it is an example of how good intentions can lead to bad outcomes, and unfortunately, it applies to other scenarios in real life, not just hypothetical prisoners.

But in real scenarios, the game is often iterated; that is, the same players face each other over and over, so they have the opportunity to learn, react, and communicate, at least implicitly. The iterated version of the game is not as easy to analyze; it is not obvious what the optimal strategy is or even whether one exists.

So in the late 1970s, Robert Axelrod organized a tournament to compare strategies. He invited participants to submit strategies in the form of computer programs, then played the programs against each other and kept score.

I won't tell you the outcome, and if you don't know, you should resist the temptation to look it up. Instead, I encourage you to run your own tournament. I'll provide the referee; you provide the players.

Exercise 10-5.

Download *http://thinkcomplex.com/Referee.py*, which runs the tournament, and *http://thinkcomplex.com/PlayerFlipper.py*, which implements a simple player strategy.

Here is the code from `PlayerFlipper.py`:

```
def move(history):
    mine, theirs = history
    if len(mine) % 2 == 0:
        return 'C'
    else:
        return 'D'
```

Any file that matches the pattern `Player*.py` is recognized as a player. The file should contain a definition for `move`, which takes the history of the match so far and returns a string: `'D'` for defect and `'C'` for cooperate.

`history` is a pair of lists: the first list contains the player's previous responses in order, and the second contains the opponent's responses.

`PlayerFlipper` checks whether the number of previous rounds is even or odd and returns `'C'` or `'D'` respectively.

Write a `move` function in a file like `PlayerFlipper.py`, but replace "Flipper" with a name that summarizes your strategy.

Run `Referee.py` and see how your strategy does.

After you run your own tournament, you can read about the results of Axelrod's tournament in his book, *The Evolution of Cooperation*.

Emergence

The examples in this chapter have something in common: emergence. An **emergent property** is a characteristic of a system that results from the interaction of its components, not from their properties.

To clarify what emergence is, it helps to consider what it isn't. For example, a brick wall is hard because bricks and mortar are hard, so that's not an emergent property. As another example, some rigid structures are built from flexible components, so that seems like a kind of emergence. But it is at best a weak kind, because structural properties follow from well-understood laws of mechanics.

Emergent properties are surprising: it is hard to predict the behavior of the system even if we know all the rules. That difficulty is not an accident; it may be the defining characteristic of emergence.

As Wolfram discusses in *A New Kind of Science*, conventional science is based on the axiom that if you know the rules that govern a system, you can predict its behavior. What we call "laws" are often computational shortcuts that allow us to predict the outcome of a system without building or observing it.

But many cellular automata are **computationally irreducible**, which means that there are no shortcuts. The only way to get the outcome is to implement the system.

The same may be true of complex systems in general. For physical systems with more than a few components, there is usually no model that yields an analytic solution. Numerical methods provide a kind of computational shortcut, but there is still a qualitative difference. Analytic solutions often provide a constant-time algorithm for prediction; that is, the runtime of the computation does not depend on t, the time scale of prediction. But numerical methods, simulation, analog computation, and similar methods take time proportional to t. In addition for many systems, there is a bound on t beyond which we can't compute reliable predictions at all.

These observations suggest that emergent properties are fundamentally unpredictable and that for complex systems, we should not expect to find natural laws in the form of computational shortcuts.

To some people, "emergence" is another name for ignorance; by this reckoning, a property is emergent if we don't have a reductionist explanation for it, but if we come to understand it better in the future, it would no longer be emergent.

The status of emergent properties is a topic of debate, so it is appropriate to be skeptical. When we see an apparently emergent property, we should not assume that there can never be a reductionist explanation. But neither should we assume that there has to be one. The examples in this book and the principle of computational equivalence give good reasons to believe that at least some emergent properties can never be explained by a classical reductionist model.

You can read more about emergence at *http://en.wikipedia.org/wiki/Emergence*.

Free Will

Many complex systems have properties as a whole that their components do not:

- The Rule 30 cellular automaton is deterministic, and the rules that govern its evolution are completely known. Nevertheless, it generates a sequence that is statistically indistinguishable from random.

- The agents in Schelling's model are not racist, but the outcome of their interactions looks as if they were.

- Traffic jams move backward even though the cars in them are moving forward.
- The behavior of flocks and herds emerges from local interactions between their members.
- As Axelrod says about the iterated Prisoner's Dilemma, "The emergence of cooperation can be explained as a consequence of individual[s] pursuing their own interests."

These examples suggest an approach to several old and challenging questions, including the problems of consciousness and free will.

Free will is the ability to make choices, but if our bodies and brains are governed by deterministic physical laws, our actions would be determined. Arguments about free will are innumerable; I will only mention two:

- William James proposed a two-stage model in which possible actions are generated by a random process and then selected by a deterministic process. In that case, our actions are fundamentally unpredictable because the process that generates them includes a random element.
- David Hume suggested that our perception of making choices is an illusion; in that case, our actions are deterministic because the system that produces them is deterministic.

These arguments reconcile the conflict in opposite ways, but they agree that there is a conflict: the system cannot have free will if the parts are deterministic.

The complex systems in this book suggest the alternative that free will, at the level of options and decisions, is compatible with determinism at the level of neurons (or some lower level). In the same way that a traffic jam moves backward while the cars move forward, a person can have free will even though neurons don't.

Exercise 10-6.

Read more about free will at *http://en.wikipedia.org/wiki/Free_will*. The view that free will is compatible with determinism is called **compatibilism**. One of the strongest challenges to compatibilism is the consequence argument.

What is the consequence argument? What response can you give to the consequence argument based on what you have read in this book?

Exercise 10-7.

In the philosophy of mind, **Strong AI** is the position that an appropriately programmed computer could have a mind in the same sense that humans have minds.

John Searle presented a thought experiment called The Chinese Room, intended to show that Strong AI is false. You can read about it at *http://en.wikipedia.org/wiki/Chinese_room*.

What is the **system reply** to the Chinese Room argument? How does what you have learned about complexity science influence your reaction to the system response?

CHAPTER 11

Case Study: Sugarscape

Dan Kearney, Natalie Mattison, and Theo Thompson

The Original Sugarscape

Sugarscape is an agent-based model developed by Joshua M. Epstein and Robert Axtell to investigate the economics of wealth distribution. They presented the original model in their book, *Growing Artificial Societies*.

The sugarscape is a virtual 2D grid where each cell has a certain amount of abstract wealth, called sugar. Agents roam the grid and accumulate sugar.

In the simplest sugarscape, each agent has a sugar reserve, a metabolism at which rate it consumes its sugar, and a range of nearby cells that it can observe. At each time step, the agent observes its nearby cells and moves to the cell with the most sugar. These rules can be expanded to include topics as varied as reproduction, death, disease, loans, and warfare. For example, a disease can be introduced to the system wherein a sick agent can infect nearby healthy agents.

Despite its simplicity, the model generates outcomes that resemble the real world. When modeling wealth with Sugarscape, a long-tailed distribution appears where some agents are vastly richer than others. Similar behavior is seen in most real economies where a small part of the population holds a large fraction of the wealth. Extreme wealth inequality is generally considered a problem, because it means there are many people barely surviving while others are fabulously rich.

The Occupy Movement

Wealth inequality has partly fueled a modern social movement known as the Occupy movement. The first significant Occupy protest was on Wall Street in New York City, where thousands of protesters gathered to express their dismay with the distribution of wealth, among other things. The movement's motto is "We are the 99%," reminding politicians to serve the majority, not the 1% who control more than a third of the nation's wealth. A major goal of the movement is to achieve a more equal distribution of income, which protesters hope to accomplish by implementing a more progressive tax policy.

One of the effects of taxation is to redistribute wealth from the rich to the poor. But opponents of the Occupy movement (and many fiscal conservatives) claim that high tax rates for the rich actually hurt the population as a whole. The logic is that wealthy people employ the poor, redistributing the wealth without the need for tax levies.

A New Take on Sugarscape

Our implementation of Sugarscape aims to study the effect of taxation on the wealth of a society. We want to show how extreme under- or over-taxation can affect the society and its individual agents, and what happens in between these two extremes. The model tests a flat tax system where every agent gets taxed a constant rate (say 10% of its total wealth) and the tax pool is redistributed evenly among all the agents. We recreate the original sugarscape and expand on it with the end goal of determining whether it is possible to shrink the wealth gap without crippling the society.

Pygame

In the process of implementing Sugarscape, we made a GUI to better understand what was happening on the grid. The visualization of the sugarscape is done with Pygame, a set of Python modules that allows easy graphic drawing. Pygame can blit images onto the screen (see *http://en.wikipedia.org/wiki/Bit_blit*), and it has built-in methods for handling user input like mouse clicks and button presses, making it ideal for designing games or other programs that receive a lot of input.

Below is an abbreviated version of our event loop that draws the cells in the GUI at each time step. `Sugarscape.nextstep` moves every agent forward by one time step, and the rest of the code redraws the update. Redrawing the entire grid is slightly less efficient than changing existing rectangle objects, but it is a common convention for Pygame. A square is drawn for each location, and the color of the square changes based on the amount of sugar contained there. Agents are represented by circles drawn on top of their current location.

```
def event_loop(self,sugarscape):
    while True:
        sugarscape.nextstep()
        for i in range(sugarscape.length):
            for j in range(sugarscape.width):
                loc = sugarscape.get_location(i,j)
                health_color = (0, 0, loc.get_sugar_amt()/loc.get_max_sugar())
                pygame.draw.rect(self.window, healthColor,(12*i,12*j,10,10))
        pygame.display.update()
```

Users can control certain attributes of the sugarscape by moving sliders underneath the grid. A histogram, implemented using the `matplotlib` library, shows the current distribution of wealth, and text fields show certain characteristics of the distribution.

Taxation and the Leave Behind

Taxation in our implementation of Sugarscape is handled with a Government object. Every 10 time steps, the Government object collects a fraction of each agent's sugar reserve, then distributes the collected sugar to each agent equally. This transfer represents services provided by the government as well as explicit redistribution of wealth.

If opponents of the Occupy movement are correct, transferring wealth from the rich to the poor makes society as a whole less productive. According to this theory, the rich create more wealth than the poor because they can open factories, fund research, and generally make investments into the economy.

In order to simulate this effect, we need to augment the model with a mechanism of wealth creation. We implement a simple "leave behind" feature, where agents leave some sugar behind as they leave a location:

$$leave\_behind = \frac{1}{5}\left(\frac{wealth \times N}{total\_wealth}\right)^{1.1}$$

In this formula, N is the total number of agents, *wealth* is the amount of sugar each agent has, and *total_wealth* is the total sugar owned by all the agents. Agents who own a large proportion of the total wealth leave behind larger amounts of sugar, making an investment into the sugarscape and increasing the total wealth.

The Gini Coefficient

To compare the effect of taxation on wealth distribution, we need a metric that measures how distributed or flat a certain wealth distribution is. We use the Gini coefficient, which is often used in economics to measure the wealth gap (see *http://en.wikipedia .org/wiki/Gini_coefficient*). The Gini coefficient is between 0 and 1, with 0 the measurement of a perfectly uniform distribution and 1 the measurement of a distribution with complete inequality.

Figure 11-1 shows a histogram describing the wealth distribution when there is no tax system in place. For most initial conditions without taxation, the sugarscape quickly develops a long-tailed distribution of wealth, skewed to the right. In these cases, some agents die quickly, particularly in an environment with many agents or one with low sugar regrowth rate. The separation between the rich and the poor is significant, and there aren't many agents occupying the middle ground. This is seen in real life in societies where there is no tax structure and there isn't much of a middle class.

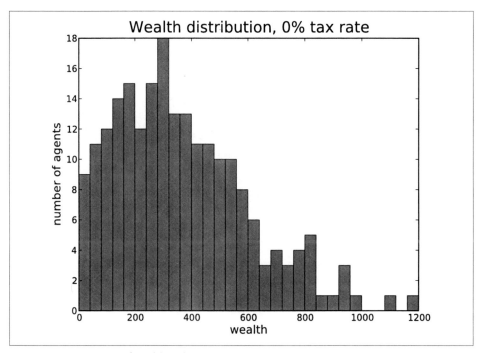

Figure 11-1. Histogram of wealth with no tax system

Results with Taxation

Figure 11-2 shows the effect of a relatively high tax rate. The agents have a similar amount of sugar, and the economy has a low Gini coefficient, 0.02.

Figure 11-3 shows that higher taxes in general result in lower Gini coefficients. This makes sense, since the point of our tax system is to redistribute wealth.

In this model, perfect equality comes at a price. With no taxation, the mean wealth was 358; with a 20% tax rate, it drops to 157. Figure 11-4 shows the effect of tax rate on wealth; mean wealth gets smaller as taxes get higher.

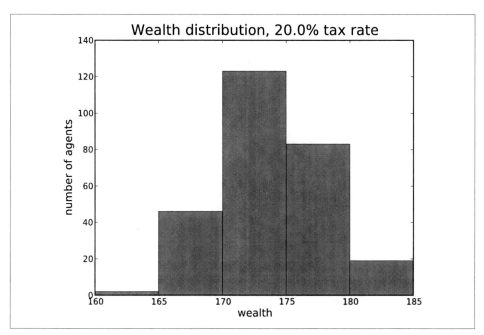

Figure 11-2. Histogram of wealth with tax system

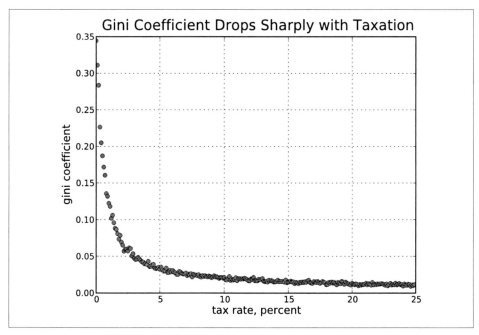

Figure 11-3. The Gini coefficient versus the tax rate

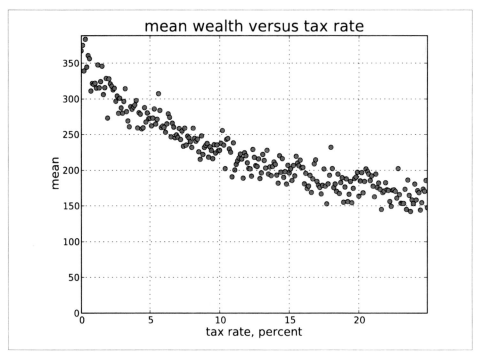

Figure 11-4. Mean wealth versus tax rate

Conclusion

It's up to a society to determine its ideal wealth distribution. In our model, there is a conflict between the goals of maximizing total wealth and minimizing inequality.

One way to reconcile this conflict is to maximize the wealth of the bottom quartile. Figure 11-5 shows the mean wealth of the poorest 25% for a range of tax rates. The optimal tax rate is around 4%. At lower rates, there is more total wealth, but the poor do not share it. At higher rates, the poor have a bigger share of a smaller pie.

Of course, this result depends on the details of our sugarscape, especially the model of productivity. But this simple model provides a way to explore relationships between wealth creation, taxation, and inequality.

Exercise 11-1.

You can download our implementation of Sugarscape from *http://thinkcomplex.com/ Sugarscape.zip*. Launch it by running `Gui.py`. The sliders allow you to control the parameters of the simulation. Experiment with these parameters to see what effect they have on the distribution of wealth.

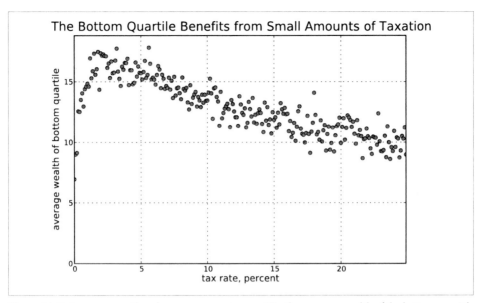

Figure 11-5. Bottom quartile value versus tax rate—at 4%, the average wealth of the bottom quartile is maximized

CHAPTER 12

Case Study: Ant Trails

Chloe Vilain and Andrew Pikler

Introduction

In nature, ants scavenge for food as a swarm. They choose their paths from the nest based on pheromone density, favoring paths with higher concentrations of a pheromone. Individuals lay pheromone trails upon finding food, allowing other members of their colony to follow them passively to the food source. Because paths leading to food have higher pheromone density, increasing numbers of ants choose these successful paths. As a result, ant trails transition over time from random paths to streamlined routes. This organization and appearance of patterns over time is an example of emergence, the process by which complex systems and patterns arise from a multiplicity of simple systems.

Ant feeding patterns lend themselves to simulation with agent-based models, which simulate the actions and interactions of autonomous agents to assess their effects on the system as a whole. When we model ant feeding patterns, each ant is an agent in the model, a self-governing individual that makes decisions based on its surroundings. When simulating large numbers of ants, behavior emerges that is reflective of ant behavior in the natural world. Beyond being intrinsically fascinating, such models have applications in the real world in areas ranging from city planning to film production.

Model Overview

We can see one example of an agent-based model in Deneuborg et al.'s 1989 paper, "The Blind Leading the Blind: Modeling Chemically Mediated Army Ant Raid Patterns," available from *http://www.ulb.ac.be/sciences/use/publications/JLD/58.pdf*.

The premise of the model is that as ants move around, they deposit a pheromone, which increases the likelihood that other ants will follow the same path. Ants that have found food lay more pheromone than ants that haven't, making it likely that other ants will follow their paths to find more food.

The ants live in a two-dimensional world of discrete points arranged in a grid. At each step of the model, each ant has a certain probability of moving to one of two neighboring coordinates in the direction the ant is facing away from the nest—forward left or forward right (see Figure 12-1). All ants start in a corner of the world, which we call the *nest*; at each time step of the simulation, we add more ants to the nest. This leads to a constant stream of outgoing ants.

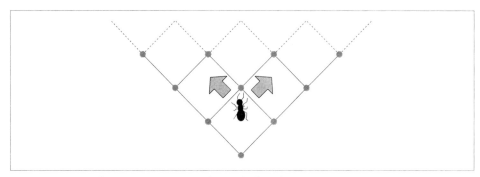

Figure 12-1. At each time step, ants move forward left or forward right

Once an ant has found food, it turns back toward the nest. It obeys the same rules for motion—that is, in each time step, its choice to move either forward left or forward right is influenced by the amounts of pheromone it sees, except now, these choices take it back toward the nest. Also, after moving, the ant lays more pheromone than it did while foraging for food. This significantly increases the probability that other foraging ants will follow its path to find, potentially, more food.

In its starting configuration, each point in the world has a chance of containing food. Once this starting condition has been set, we let the simulation run for about 1000 time steps and plot the result. You can see the plot of one such simulation in Figure 12-2, which is similar to the actual foraging patterns Deneuborg et al. present in their Figure 1.

Exercise 12-1.

Download the code for our simulation from *http://thinkcomplex.com/ants.py*. Run it for 1000 time steps, and see if your results look similar to Figure 12-2. The simulation can be computationally intensive; 1000 time steps took almost two minutes on our computer, so be patient!

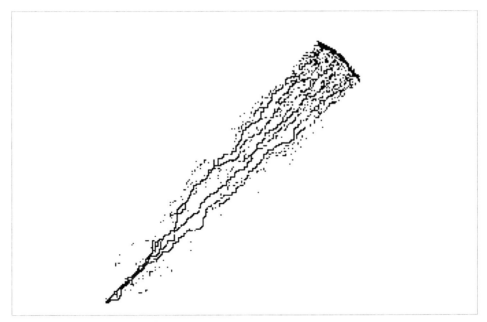

Figure 12-2. The simulation after 1000 time steps

API Design

The challenges of writing a simulation such as this include designing classes that are easy for human readers of the code to understand, and implementing data structures that allow the code to execute efficiently.

One way to break up a model into classes is to list the main nouns you use when describing the model, and then represent the most prominent of those nouns as objects. In our model, the primary objects are the World, which contains Ants, and Locations that represent points in the grid.

The next step is to decide what information about the current state each class is responsible for. In our case, the behavior of the World is defined by what Ants and Locations can do, so it makes sense to design our classes bottom-up and consider the World only once we have at least a tentative idea for the methods and attributes of Ants and Locations.

For Ants, the most important information is where they are in the World, so each ant has the attributes x and y to store its coordinates. Also, each Ant keeps track of whether or not it is currently carrying food. Each Ant has only local information about the World; keeping track of all the Ants is the job of the World object itself.

Ants provide two methods that the World uses to interact with them:

getPos
> Returns the current coordinates of this Ant

move
> Collects local information and moves the Ant accordingly

Locations know even less than Ants; each Location only keeps track of the food and pheromone it contains. Locations provide accessor methods that Ants and the World use to modify the Location's food and pheromone amounts.

Locations do not keep track of their coordinates on the map, because they never change. Instead, this information is represented implicitly by a dictionary that maps from coordinates to Location objects.

There is only one World object; this instance keeps track of all existing Ants and Locations. The World provides methods for controlling the state of the simulation: move_ants advances the simulation by one time step by calling every existing Ant's move method and evaporating a proportion of pheromone from each Location. Other methods include add_ants, which adds a specified number of ants to the nest; place_food, which puts food at each Location with some probability; and get_location, which looks up the Location at given coordinates.

Sparse Matrices

The group of Locations that make up our World is implemented as a **sparse matrix**. In this representation, Locations don't exist until they are needed; World.get_location is responsible for fetching either the existing Location at the given coordinates, or creating a new Location if it doesn't exist.

An alternate implementation would be a **dense matrix**, either a Python list of lists or a NumPy array. In our case, the sparse matrix has two advantages:

- Since most of the World is empty most of the time, it is more memory-efficient to only keep track of those Locations that aren't empty.
- A sparse matrix doesn't have preset boundaries, so an Ant is free to wander off in any direction. It would be more difficult to implement this feature with a dense matrix.

WX

We use the wx Python package to plot a picture of the ants after the simulation finishes running.

We define a class called AntPlot, which takes a World, creates a wx window, and plots the ants (see Figure 12-2):

```
class AntPlot:
    def __init__(self, world):
        self.world = world
        self.app = wx.PySimpleApp()
        self.w = 500
        self.h = 500
        self.frame = wx.Frame(None, -1, 'Ant Plot', size=(self.w, self.h))
        self.canvas = FloatCanvas(self.frame, -1)


    def draw(self):
        positions = self.world.get_ant_dict()
        for pos in positions:
            x, y = pos
            x -= self.w / 2
            y -= self.h / 2
            self.canvas.AddPoint((x, y))
        self.frame.Show()
        self.app.MainLoop()
```

We use a wx FloatCanvas to plot the ants. Most canvases in GUI libraries define the point (0, 0) as the upper-left corner of the canvas and have x increase to the left and y increase down, but the coordinates in the FloatCanvas work like in math—the origin is the middle, and the positive y direction is up. This allows us to write simpler code because we don't have to transform our coordinates to the canvas's system.

If you are interested in exploring wx further, AntPlot might be a good starting point.

Exercise 12-2.

To understand the behavior of the model better, make some changes and see what effect they have. For example, try altering the pheromone amounts in the model. What happens when Ants deposit significantly more or less pheromone? What happens when Ants only lay pheromone when leaving the nest, or only when returning?

Exercise 12-3.

The distribution of food affects the structure of the trails. In ant.py, each Location has a 50% probability of containing one particle of food. What happens when each Location has a 1% probability of containing 50 pieces of food?

Exercise 12-4.

So far, we have modeled one nest of ants. What happens with multiple nests? Pick a value, d, and modify the code such that Ants spawn at $(0, d)$ and $(d, 0)$ in addition to $(0,0)$. Do the trails of Ants converge, or do they all remain distinct?

Keep track of the amount of food collected in each nest. Does one of the nests do better than the others?

What happens when ants from one nest lay slightly higher amounts of pheromone than those from the other nests?

Applications

Agent-based models have numerous applications, from modeling traffic patterns to creating realistic battle simulations. The entertainment industry uses agent-based models to simulate crowds in films, games, and advertisements.

This kind of modeling is more scalable than filming; it is easier to simulate a large crowd than to recruit thousands of extras. Agent-based models make it feasible to create large-scale, visually stunning sequences.

The *Lord of the Rings* trilogy is a salient example. Visual effects developers were tasked with creating battles with hundreds of thousands of soldiers from a variety of races with different fighting techniques. They implemented an agent-based model where each agent had about 200 possible motions (animated using motion capture). Agents followed simple rules to choose possible responses based on logic and probabilities. Different races—elves, orcs, and men—were based on the same "master agent" but had different weapons, abilities, and programmed attack responses.

Simulating thousands of agents in tandem allowed for exceptionally complex battle sequences. The results sometimes surprised even the programmers—in one simulation, a number of agents fled the battle. They were not programmed to flee; that is, fleeing was not explicitly an option. Rather, this behavior emerged from the interaction of agents following simple rules. This unexpected action, which would be realistic in an actual battle scenario, demonstrates the power of agent-based models.

The software developed for the trilogy, called Massive, has become the industry standard for simulating large-scale battle sequences. Massive has since been used for battle sequences in movies like *Chronicles of Narnia* and *300*, and for more benign crowd simulations in *Happy Feet* and *Avatar*.

The models used in these films are more complicated than our simulated ant trails, but they are examples of the same concept. Like the agents in *Lord of the Rings*, our Ants follow simple rules, but their iteractions yield realistic, complex, and sometimes unpredictable behavior.

CHAPTER 13

Case Study: Directed Graphs and Knots

Rachel Bobbins and Noam Rubin

Directed Graphs

Imagine that it's 2 a.m. during finals week, and you're scrambling to finish a research paper on *topica obscura*. Your adrenaline jumps when you find a relevant Wikipedia article, with links to more Wikipedia articles! You start clicking away, jumping from page to page in search of facts. An hour later, you realize you're still clicking, but these are pages you've already visited. No matter which link you click, you can't seem to discover any new pages!

If this has happened to you, you've unknowingly (and unfortunately) stumbled upon a knot in Wikipedia. Knots are a unique property of directed graphs. To understand them, it is necessary to have a basic understanding of directed graphs.

The graphs in the rest of this book are undirected. In an undirected graph, an edge represents a symmetric relationship between vertices. This abstraction is appropriate for some applications (such as acquaintance networks and transportation networks), but other applications involve asymmetric relationships (for example, links between pages in the World Wide Web).

Wikipedia links are also asymmetric. Page A might link to page B, but page B doesn't have to include any links to page A. To fully describe the relationship between pages A and B, we need two bits of information: whether A links to B, and whether B links to A. This is the essence of a directed graph. In a directed graph, a directed edge, $e = (A, B)$, is an edge from A to B.

Knots are a unique (and sometimes cruel) property of directed graphs. A knot is a collection of vertices and edges with the property that every vertex in the knot has outgoing edges, and all outgoing edges from vertices in the knot terminate at other vertices in the knot. Thus, it is impossible to leave the knot while following any path along its directed edges.

Implementation

In the scenario above, we imagined finding a knot in Wikipedia; that is, a set of articles with links to each other, but no links to other articles.

We wondered whether such a thing was even possible. Given that there are 3,811,000+ articles on Wikipedia and they all link to different pages, it seemed unlikely that there would be a knot, but we decided to investigate.

We started by extending Graph.py, from "Representing Graphs" on page 13, to support directed graphs. The result is DirectedGraph.py, which you can download from *http://thinkcomplex.com/DirectedGraph.py*.

When we were designing DirectedGraph, we wanted to preserve the order of growth of Vertex and Arc lookups as they were in Graph. However, we needed to keep track of edges into a vertex and edges from a vertex. It made sense to keep track of these in separate dictionaries. Having two dictionaries takes twice as much memory, but this is a reasonable price to pay for maintaining the speed of lookups.

Detecting Knots

To detect knots in a directed graph, we developed an algorithm based on a breadth-first-search. _bfsknots searches for all the vertices that can be reached from a given starting vertex, and returns these vertices as a set:

```python
def _bfsknots(self, s):
    # initialize the queue with the start vertex
    queue = [s]
    visited = set()
    on_first_vertex = True
    while queue:

        # get the next vertex
        v = queue.pop(0)

        # skip it if it's already marked
        if v in visited: continue

        # if we're on the first vertex, we're not actually visiting
        if v != s or not on_first_vertex: visited.add(v)
        on_first_vertex = False

        for x in self.out_vertices(v):
            #if its out vertices have been cached, update visited
            if x in self._knot_cache.keys():
                visited.update(self._knot_cache[x])
                visited.add(x)
```

```
              #otherwise add it to the queue
              elif x not in self._knot_cache.keys():
                  queue.append(x)

       return visited
```

We run _bfsknots for every vertex in the graph and build a dictionary that maps from a vertex to the set of vertices it can reach; that is, for each vertex, V, we know the set of reachable vertices, S_V.

If there is a knot in the graph, then for every vertex, V, in the knot, the reachable set S_V is exactly the set of vertices in the knot.

The function has_knot iterates through each vertex in a graph and returns true if this condition holds. If it checks the whole graph and does not find a knot, it returns false:

```
def has_knot(self):
    """
    Returns true if directed graph has a knot.
    """
    self._knot_cache = {}
    #build the cache of which vertices are accessible from which
    for v in self:
        self._knot_cache[v] = self._bfsknots(v)

    #searches for knot
    for v in self:
        if self._knot_at_v(v):
            return True
    return False
```

Finally, _knot_at_v checks whether all vertices reachable from V have the reachable set S_V.

Exercise 13-1.

Download *http://thinkcomplex.com/DirectedGraph.py*. Read through the file to make yourself familiar with the terminology. Note that edges in DirectedGraph are represented by Arcs.

Determine the order of growth of has_knots experimentally. You can follow the example in "Summing Lists" on page 31. Below are some hints to help you out:

1. Use DirectedGraph.add_random_edges to generate graphs of different sizes.
2. For each graph, time how long it takes to check whether it has a knot.
3. On a log-log scale, plot runtime versus the number of vertices and runtime versus the number of edges.

Exercise 13-2.

Find all the knots in a directed graph.

1. Write a function, `all_knots`, that returns a list of all knots in a graph, where each knot is a set of vertices.

2. Write a function named `entry_points` that returns a list of all the vertices that serve as entry points into knots.

Knots in Wikipedia

To find knots in Wikipedia, we selected 558 disjoint subsets of Wikipedia articles, organized by index. For example, the index of articles about neurobiology was used to define one subset, and the index of articles about Zimbabwe was used to define another subset. The 558 subsets contain about 321,000 articles, or 10% of Wikipedia.

Of these subsets we examined, 38% contained at least one knot. So if you are restricted to articles listed on a single index page, there is a substantial chance you will eventually find a knot.

For the complete Wikipedia, the probability is lower because articles can link to articles in other indices. Based on these results, we cannot say yet whether the complete Wikipedia has a knot.

When you started your hypothetical research on *topica obscura*, you might have used journal articles instead of Wikipedia articles. Instead of links, you would have used citations to find other papers.

In that case, you would never find a knot. Why not? Because science articles are published sequentially, and a paper cannot cite a paper that will be created in the future. So the directed graph that represents papers and their citations cannot have a knot.

CHAPTER 14

Case Study: The Volunteer's Dilemma

Molly Grossman, Mandy Korpusik, and Philip Loh

The Prairie Dog's Dilemma

Suppose you are a prairie dog assigned to guard duty with other prairie dogs from your town. When you see a predator coming, you have two choices: sound the alarm or remain silent. If you sound the alarm, you help ensure the safety of the other prairie dogs, but you also encourage the predator to come after you. For you, it is safer to remain silent, but if all guards remain silent, everyone is less safe, including you. What should you do when you see a predator?

This scenario is an example of the Volunteer's Dilemma, a game similar to the Prisoner's Dilemma discussed in "Prisoner's Dilemma" on page 102. In the Prisoner's Dilemma, each player has two options: cooperate and defect. In the Volunteer's Dilemma, each player also has two options: volunteer (sound the alarm in our prairie dog example) or ignore (remain silent). If one player volunteers, then the other player is better off ignoring. But if both players ignore, both pay a high cost.

In the Prisoner's Dilemma, both players are better off if they both cooperate; however, since neither knows what the other will do, each independently comes to the conclusion that he or she should defect.

In the Volunteer's Dilemma, it is not immediately clear what outcome is best for both players. Suppose the players are named Alice and Bob. If Alice volunteers, Bob is better off ignoring; if Alice ignores, Bob is better off volunteering. This does not provide a clear best strategy for Bob. By the same analysis, Alice reaches the same conclusion: if Bob volunteers, she is better off ignoring; and if Bob ignores, she is better off volunteering.

Instead of one optimal outcome, as in the Prisoner's Dilemma, there are two equally good outcomes: Bob volunteers and Alice ignores, or Bob ignores and Alice volunteers.

In the prairie dog town, there are more than two guards. As in the scenario with just Alice and Bob, only one player needs to volunteer to benefit the entire town. So there are as many good outcomes as guards—in each case, one guard volunteers and the others ignore.

If one guard is always going to volunteer, though, then there is little point in having multiple guards. To make the situation more fair, we can allow the guards to distribute the burden of volunteering among themselves by making decisions randomly; that is, each guard chooses to ignore with some probability γ or to volunteer with probability $1-\gamma$. The optimal value for γ is where each player volunteers as little as necessary to produce the common good.

Analysis

Marco Archetti investigates the optimal value of γ in his paper "The Volunteer's Dilemma and the Optimal Size of a Social Group" (*http://people.fas.harvard.edu/~archetti/papers/JTB_2009_VD.pdf*). This section replicates his analysis.

When each player volunteers with the optimal probability, the expected payoff of volunteering is the same as the expected payoff of ignoring. Were the payoff of volunteering higher than the payoff of ignoring, the player would volunteer more often and ignore less; the opposite would be true were the payoff of ignoring higher than the payoff of volunteering.

The optimal probability depends on the costs and benefits of each option. In fact, the optimal γ for two individuals is:

$$\gamma_2 = c / a$$

where c is the cost of volunteering and a is the total cost if nobody volunteers. In the prairie dog example, where the damage of nobody volunteering is high, γ_2 is small.

If you transfer more prairie dogs to guard duty, there are more players to share the cost of volunteering, so we expect the probability of each player ignoring should increase. Indeed, Archetti shows:

$$\gamma_N = \gamma_2^{1/(N-1)}$$

γ_N increases with N, so as the number of players increases, each player volunteers less.

But surprisingly, adding more guards does not make the town safer. If everyone volunteers at the optimal probability, the probability that everyone except you ignores is γ_N^{N-1}, which is γ_2, so it doesn't depend on N. If you also ignore with probability γ_N, the probability that everyone ignores is $\gamma_2\gamma_N$, which *increases* with N.

This result is disheartening. We can ensure that the high-damage situation never occurs by placing the entire burden of the common good on one individual who must volunteer all the time. We could instead be more fair and distribute the burden of volunteering among the players by asking each of them to volunteer some percentage of the time, but the high-damage situation will occur more frequently as the number of players who share the burden increases.

Exercise 14-1.

Read about the bystander effect at *http://en.wikipedia.org/wiki/Bystander_effect*. What explanation, if any, does the Volunteer's Dilemma provide for the bystander effect?

Exercise 14-2.

Some colleges have an honor code that requires students to report instances of cheating. If a student cheats on an exam, other students who witness the infraction face a version of the Volunteer's Dilemma. As a witness, you have two options: report the offender or ignore. If you report, you help maintain the integrity of the honor code and the college's culture of honesty and integrity, but you incur costs, including strained relationships and emotional discomfort. If someone else reports, you benefit without the stress and hassle. But if everyone ignores, the integrity of the honor code is diminished, and if cheaters are not punished, other students might be more likely to cheat.

Download and run *http://thinkcomplex.com/volunteersDilemma.py*, which contains a basic implementation of the Volunteer's Dilemma. The code plots the likelihood that nobody will volunteer with given values of c and a across a range of values for N. Edit this code to investigate the honor code Volunteer's Dilemma. How does the probability of nobody volunteering change as you modify the cost of volunteering, the cost of nobody volunteering, and the size of the population?

The Norms Game

At some colleges, cheating is commonplace and students seldom report cheaters. At other colleges, cheating is rare and likely to be reported and punished. The explicit and implicit rules about cheating and reporting cheaters are **social norms**.

Social norms influence the behavior of individuals: for example, you might be more likely to cheat if you think it is common and seldom punished. But individuals also influence social norms: if more people report cheaters, fewer people will cheat. We can extend the analysis from the previous section to model these effects.

Our model is based on a genetic algorithm presented by Robert Axelrod in "An Evolutionary Approach to Norms" (*http://www.jstor.org/stable/1960858*). Genetic algorithms model the process of natural evolution. We create a population of simulated individuals with different attributes. The individuals interact in ways that test their fitness (by some definition of "fitness"). Individuals with higher fitness are more likely to reproduce, so over time, the average fitness of the population increases.

In the cheating scenario, the relevant attributes are:

Boldness
    The likelihood that an individual cheats

Vengefulness
    The likelihood that an individual reports a cheater

The players interact by playing two games, called "cheat-or-not" and "punish-or-not." In the first, each player decides whether to cheat, depending on the value of *boldness*. In the second, each player decides whether to report a cheater, depending on *vengefulness*. These subgames are played several times per generation, so each player has several opportunities to cheat and punish cheaters.

The fitness of each player depends on how they play the subgames. When a player cheats, his fitness increases by *reward* points, but the fitness of others decreases by *damage* points. Each individual who reports a cheater loses *cost* fitness points and causes the cheater to lose *punishment* fitness points.

At the end of each generation, individuals with the highest fitness levels have the most children in the next generation. The properties of each individual in the new generation are then mutated to maintain variation.

This code summarizes the structure of the simulation:

```
for generations in range(many):
    for steps in range(repetitions):
        for person in persons:
            cheat_or_not()
            punish_or_not()
    genetic_repopulation()
    genetic_mutation()
```

Results

Each run starts with a random population and runs for 300 generations. The parameters of the simulation are *reward* = 3, *damage* = 1, *cost* = 2, *punishment* = 9. At the end, we compute the mean boldness and vengefulness of the population. Figure 14-1 shows the results; each dot represents one run of the simulation.

There are two clear clusters, one with low boldness and one with high boldness. When boldness is low, the average vengefulness is spread out, which suggests that vengefulness does not matter very much. If few people cheat, opportunities to punish are rare and the effect of vengefulness on fitness is small. When boldness is high, vengefulness is consistently low.

In the low-boldness cluster, average fitness is higher, so individuals in the high-boldness cluster would be better off if they could move. But if they make a unilateral move toward higher boldness or higher vengefulness, their fitness suffers. So the high-boldness scenario is stable, which is why this cluster exists.

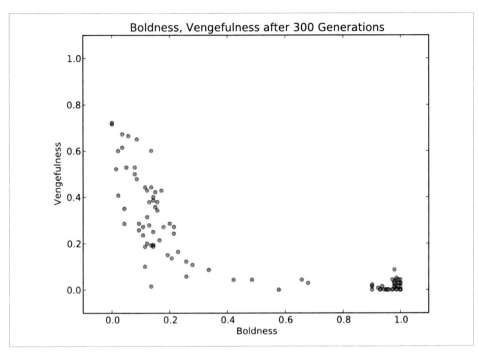

Figure 14-1. End conditions after 300 generations

Improving the Chances

Suppose you are founding a new college and thinking about the academic culture you want to create. You probably prefer an environment where cheating is rare. But our simulations suggest that there are two stable outcomes, with low and high rates of cheating. What can you do to improve the chances of reaching (and staying in) the low-cheating regime?

The parameters of the simulation affect the probability of the outcomes. In the previous section, the parameters were *reward* = 3, *damage* = 1, *cost* = 2, *punishment* = 9. The probability of reaching the low-cheating regime was about 50%. If you were founding a new college, you might not like those odds.

The parameters that have the strongest effect on the outcome are *cost*, the cost of reporting a cheater, and *punishment*, the cost of getting caught. Figure 14-2 shows how the proportion of good outcomes depends on these parameters.

There are two ways to increase the chances of a good outcome: decreasing *cost* or increasing *punishment*. If we fix *punishment* = 9 and decrease *cost* to 1, the probability of a good outcome is 80%. If we fix *cost* = 2, to achieve the same probability, we have to increase *punishment* to 11.

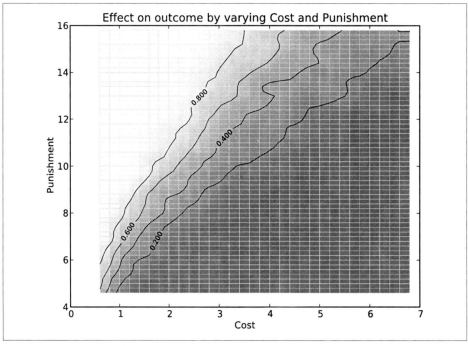

Figure 14-2. Proportion of good outcomes, varying the cost of reporting cheaters and the punishment for cheating

Which option is more appealing depends on practical and cultural considerations. Of course, we have to be careful not to take this model too seriously. It is a highly abstracted model of complex human behavior. Nevertheless, it provides insight into the emergence and stability of social norms.

Exercise 14-3.

In this section, we fixed *reward* and *damage*, and explored the effect of *cost* and *punishment*. Download our code from *http://thinkcomplex.com/normsGame.py*, and run it to replicate these results.

Then modify it to explore the effect of *reward* and *damage*. With the other parameters fixed, what values of *reward* and *damage* give a 50% chance of reaching a good outcome? What about 70% and 90%?

Exercise 14-4.

The games in this case study are based on work in game theory, which is a set of mathematical methods for analyzing the behavior of agents who follow simple rules in response to economic costs and benefits. You can read more about game theory at *http://en.wikipedia.org/wiki/Game_theory*.

Call for Submissions

The case studies in this book were written by students at Olin College, and edited by Lisa Downey and Allen Downey. They were reviewed by a program committee of faculty at Olin College who chose the ones that met the criteria of interest and quality. I am grateful to the program committee and the students.

I invite readers to submit additional case studies. Reports that meet the criteria will be published in an online supplement to this book, and the best of them will be included in future print editions.

The criteria are the following:

- The case study should be relevant to complexity. For an overview of possible topics, see *http://en.wikipedia.org/wiki/Complexity* and *http://en.wikipedia.org/wiki/Complex_systems*. Topics not already covered in the book are particularly welcome.

- A good case study might present a seminal paper, reimplement an important experiment, discuss the results, and explain their context. Original research is not necessary and might not be appropriate for this format, but you could extend existing results.

- A good case study should invite the reader to participate by including exercises, references to further reading, and topics for discussion.

- The case study should present enough technical detail that the reader could implement the model in a language like Python.

- If you use an algorithm or data structure that deserves comment, you should discuss it. Topics not covered in the book, including tree algorithms and dynamic programming, are particularly welcome.

- If you use a feature of Python or a module that you think will interest readers, you should discuss it. But you should stick to modules that are in widespread use and either included in Python distributions or easy to install.

For more details, see *http://thinkcomplex.com/case_studies*.

Reading List

In my class, we start the semester by reading popular books about complexity science. They provide a pleasant way to get a big picture of the field and start to see connections between topics.

One problem with these books is that they are written for a non-technical audience, so after a while the students get frustrated by the vagueness and hand-waving. That's what *this* book is for.

The other problem is that students can't read 30 books in a week, or even a semester. Instead, I provide one copy of each book and ask the students to pick one, read the first chapter, write a summary, and post it on the class web page.

During the next class session, the students swap books. Each student reads the summary written by the previous student, then reads the next chapter, and writes a summary.

After a few iterations, we have a class discussion where students report what they have read so far and we look for connections. For example, one student might present a topic, then another student suggests a related topic and explains the relationship. I draw the topics and the relationships between them on the board (see *http://en.wikipedia.org/wiki/Concept_map*).

We repeat this exercise until we have seen what there is to see, or we are impatient to get down to business.

You can see the list of books and read the summaries my students wrote at *https://sites.google.com/site/compmodolin*.

Here are the books:

- Axelrod, *Complexity of Cooperation*
- Axelrod, *The Evolution of Cooperation*
- Bak, *How Nature Works*
- Barabasi, *Linked*

- Buchanan, *Nexus*
- Epstein and Axtell, *Growing Artificial Societies: Social Science from the Bottom Up*
- Fisher, *The Perfect Swarm*
- Flake, *The Computational Beauty of Nature*
- Goodwin, *How the Leopard Changed Its Spots*
- Holland, *Hidden Order*
- Johnson, *Emergence*
- Kelly, *Out of Control*
- Kluger, *Simplexity*
- Levy, *Artificial Life*
- Lewin, *Complexity: Life at the Edge of Chaos*
- Mitchell, *Complexity: A Guided Tour*
- Mitchell Waldrop, *Complexity: the emerging science at the edge of order and chaos*
- Resnick, *Turtles, Termites, and Traffic Jams*
- Rucker, *The Lifebox, The Seashell, and The Soul*
- Sawyer, *Social Emergence: Societies As Complex Systems*
- Schelling, *Micromotives and Macrobehaviors*
- Schiff, *Cellular Automata: A Discrete View of the World*
- Strogatz, *Sync*
- Watts, *Six Degrees*
- Wolfram, *A New Kind of Science*

Index

Symbols

+= operator, 31
1-D cellular automaton, 58
1/f noise, 87, 91, 95
2D cellular automaton, 88
80/20 rule, 49

A

abstract class, 61
abstract model, 3, 44, 55, 70, 88
agent-based model, 2, 97, 98
agents, 2
algorithms, 1, 21
all pairs shortest path, 43
amphetamine, 18
analogy, 54, 93
analysis, 7
    of algorithms, 21
    of graph algorithms, 37
    of practical algorithms, 24
    of primitives, 24
angular frequency, 89
animation, 75
Appel, Kenneth, 6
argument by analogy, 54, 70
Aristotelian logic, 8
array indexing, 60
array slice, 60
arrays, 59
asymptotic analysis, 22
avalanche model, 84, 88
average case, 22
average cost, 30
Axelrod, Robert, 103

B

badness, 23
Bak, Per, 84, 87, 94
Barabási-Albert model, 51
Bayesian, 8
becquerel, 12
beetles, 69
behavior, 54
BetterMap, 27
BFS, 17, 37, 42
Big O notation, 23
The Big Sort, 98
bin size, 46
bisect module, 26
bisection search, 26
Bishop, Bill, 98
boid, 100
bond percolation, 84
bottom-up, 7
bounded, 28
box-counting dimension, 81
breadth-first search, 17, 37, 42
brick wall, 103
broadcast service, 7
bubble sort, 21
busy beaver, 68

C

CA, 60
CADrawer, 61
caffeine, 18
canonical ensemble, 85
carrot, 100
causation, 64, 95, 97

We'd like to hear your suggestions for improving our indexes. Send email to *index@oreilly.com*.

About the Author

Allen Downey is a Professor of Computer Science at the Olin College of Engineering. He has taught computer science at Wellesley College, Colby College, and U.C. Berkeley. He has a Ph.D. in Computer Science from U.C. Berkeley, and Master's and Bachelor's degrees from MIT.

Colophon

The animal on the cover of *Think Complexity* is a black eagle (*Ictinaetus malayensis*), the only species in its genus. They are found in tropical Asia, namely parts of Burma, India, southern China, Taiwan, and the Malay peninsula. These eagles prefer wooded mountainous terrain, roosting and building large nests (3-4 feet wide) high in the trees.

These birds have black plumage (as their common name states; though juvenile eagles are dark brown), yellow feet, and a short curved beak. Black eagles are large birds averaging 2-3 feet long, with a massive wingspan of 5 feet. In flight, the eagles are distinctive not only for their color and size, but the slow gliding pace at which they move above the canopy.

Breeding season occurs sometime between November and May (depending on latitude). The eagles carry out aerial displays of a steep dive followed by an ascent, all at high speed. Mating pairs will also chase each other among the trees. They typically only lay one or two eggs at a time. The diet of the black eagle is made up of small mammals (which they will capture from the ground), as well as smaller birds and eggs.

In fact, black eagles are voracious nest-predators, and have a unique hunting habit—picking up an entire nest of prey and carrying the eggs or nestlings away to its own perch to eat later. Because the black eagle's talons are less sharply curved than other birds of prey, it is easier for them to accomplish this.

The cover image is from *Meyers Konversations-Lexikon*, 3rd edition. The cover font is Adobe ITC Garamond. The text font is Linotype Birka; the heading font is Adobe Myriad Condensed; and the code font is LucasFont's TheSansMonoCondensed.

Have it your way.

O'Reilly eBooks

- Lifetime access to the book when you buy through oreilly.com
- Provided in up to four DRM-free file formats, for use on the devices of your choice: PDF, .epub, Kindle-compatible .mobi, and Android .apk
- Fully searchable, with copy-and-paste and print functionality
- Alerts when files are updated with corrections and additions

oreilly.com/ebooks/

Safari Books Online

- Access the contents and quickly search over 7000 books on technology, business, and certification guides
- Learn from expert video tutorials, and explore thousands of hours of video on technology and design topics
- Download whole books or chapters in PDF format, at no extra cost, to print or read on the go
- Get early access to books as they're being written
- Interact directly with authors of upcoming books
- Save up to 35% on O'Reilly print books

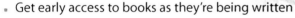

See the complete Safari Library at safari.oreilly.com

O'REILLY®

Spreading the knowledge of innovators.   oreilly.com

©2011 O'Reilly Media, Inc. O'Reilly logo is a registered trademark of O'Reilly Media, Inc. 00000

Get even more for your money.

Join the O'Reilly Community, and register the O'Reilly books you own. It's free, and you'll get:

- $4.99 ebook upgrade offer
- 40% upgrade offer on O'Reilly print books
- Membership discounts on books and events
- Free lifetime updates to ebooks and videos
- Multiple ebook formats, DRM FREE
- Participation in the O'Reilly community
- Newsletters
- Account management
- 100% Satisfaction Guarantee

Signing up is easy:

1. **Go to: oreilly.com/go/register**
2. **Create an O'Reilly login.**
3. **Provide your address.**
4. **Register your books.**

Note: English-language books only

To order books online:
oreilly.com/store

For questions about products or an order:
orders@oreilly.com

To sign up to get topic-specific email announcements and/or news about upcoming books, conferences, special offers, and new technologies:
elists@oreilly.com

For technical questions about book content:
booktech@oreilly.com

To submit new book proposals to our editors:
proposals@oreilly.com

O'Reilly books are available in multiple DRM-free ebook formats. For more information:
oreilly.com/ebooks

O'REILLY®

Spreading the knowledge of innovators
oreilly.com

©2010 O'Reilly Media, Inc. O'Reilly logo is a registered trademark of O'Reilly Media, Inc. 00000

CPSIA information can be obtained at www.ICGtesting.com
Printed in the USA
BVOW051005130812

297742BV00006B/18/P

9 781449 314637